D1290273

Sex, Drink and Fast Cars

S E X ,

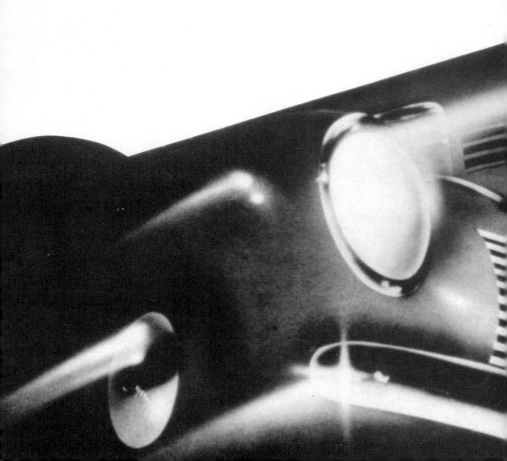

DRINK

and

FAST

CARS

STEPHEN BAYLEY

Pantheon Books New York

Library of Congress Cataloging-in-Publication Data

Bayley, Stephen.
    Sex, drink, and fast cars.

    1. Automobiles—Social aspects—United States—History. 2. Automobiles—United States—Design and construction—History. 3. Automobiles—Technological innovations—History. 4. Consumers' preferences—History. I. Title.
HD9710.U52B34   1987   303.4′832   86-42976
ISBN 0-394-75046-2

Manufactured in the United States of America

First American Edition

To Flo, Drink, Fast Cars and Bruno

CONTENTS

ACKNOWLEDGEMENTS

Some of the material in this book originally appeared, with slight differences, in the *Tatler*, the *Observer Magazine* and *Motor*. Particularly helpful in the preparation were: John Meszadros of Audi-Volkswagen; Jeremy Judge and John Hegarty of Bartle Bogle Hegarty; David Abbott of Abbott Mead Vickers; Gordon Murray of Motor Racing Developments; Dan Jones, Andy Graves and Phil Gardiner of The Science Policy Research Unit, Sussex University; Uwe Bahnsen of Ford. Helen Rees did the research.

For a list of those who kindly allowed me to quote their publications in this book please see page 111.

1 INTRODUCTION
Sex, Drink and Fast Cars

Harley Earl's 'Le Sabre' was one of the first dream cars, although it was more likely the product of an erotic, science-fiction nightmare. Named after a USAF jet, Le Sabre, with its questing forward nozzle, served as a symbol of potency for Earl in Grosse Pointe and for Dwight Eisenhower, who used it in Paris.

I had breakfast with a friend the morning after he had celebrated his fortieth birthday. He had that sense of regret coupled with the fairly profound wisdom of those who have celebrated over-well. He said to me, morosely pushing a morsel of poached haddock around his plate:

You know, Stephen, as I get older I've had to reconsider the priorities in life.

I struck the pose of a credulous martyr, but inside I was resigned to a homily about the virtues of pastoral poetry, family life, experimental communion with the Godhead and 'philosophy'. Instead, my friend said to me:

And I'm more than ever certain that they are sex, drink and fast cars.

The fantasies and aspirations and appetites of most of the world are summarized in that one bathetic sentence . . . and in the following, less subtle, but more robust one:

I just wanna race motorcycles and screw people.

That was the way Little Fauss put his *Weltanschauung* in the popular road movie, *Little Fauss and Big Halsey*. Like Little Fauss, my breakfasting friend was a North American. They are people with a peculiarly strong attachment to cars. I asked a Canadian why his continent bred a specially intense kind of car freak and he explained that, with no depth of culture and with no public transport and with an economic system which encouraged *consumption*, cars were a form of display. Every part of American life allows for more mobility than its European equivalent and it is a sort of mobility which is both real and metaphorical: money moves more freely in America. You can buy, rent, lease, hire or acquire things on credit. It is not unusual to drive 120 miles to see friends for dinner, at least in California. In a continent of shifting values, the coast-to-coast franchised trademarks provided fixed points, heraldry which consumers can readily identify. The cars provided the costumes.

It is a poetic truism that the pioneer American automobile manufacturers were farmboys who knew at first hand the crushing loneliness and mindless drudgery of life in the rural mid-West. Henry Ford wrote in his autobiography, *My Life and Work* (1922), 'It was life on the farm that drove me into devising ways and means to better transportation.' By 1980, on my own first visit to Detroit, his inheritors had exchanged life on the farm for something altogether different. I remember leaving Detroit's terrifying Renaissance Center (a name which deserves a *sic*, if ever there was one) and trying to find my way by road to a house in Grosse Pointe, the high-income Detroit suburb, where metalled roads replaced tracks made in mud by Henry's buggy. It was summer and the day had been so hot and humid that I experienced something that was, to me, entirely novel: with the air conditioning in my little Ford coupé turned on, condensation streamed down the *outside* of the car. I was driving a refrigerated tin through the prologue to a tropical storm.

By the time I had got lost and was late for dinner, that storm had broken into genuine movie special effects. Forked lightning, navy blue sky, heavy rain that pushed the wipers back. The feeble headlights could not cope, but the electrical weather helped me see white palings, white chain link and a very long gravel drive leading to the house. That description qualified me for being almost anywhere in Grosse Pointe, but good fortune had, in fact, got me to my destination. Prosperous Grosse Pointe's replacement for the farm.

I was tired and looking forward to sitting back and being a modest English observer at a Michigan society dinner. I thought that if I was noticed at all a quaint accent and some charming, untaxing observations about the characteristics separating life in the English Home Counties and Michigan would see me through to the nuts. Good fortune had ended at the terminus of the gravel: I was the only guest. I had assumed the black maid who opened the door was quivering on account of the thunder and lightning, but when I found my elegant host in a similar, but more controlled, state of nervousness I knew it was going to be a difficult dinner. In the event it was harrowing, with lots of spilling and banging; once the cutlery jumped to emphasize a point about the knavery (although that was not the word) of the English. We were surrounded by what I at first took to be prints, but later realized were real Picassos and Matisses.

It all began to make me think about the effect that cars have on people. In the case of my hosts it had clearly been an unhappy one: the great wealth accruing from Henry Ford's 'gasoline buggy' had isolated some unfortunate people in an American suburb where even the vivid heraldry that can be bought with money was not enough to compensate for a sense of loss which the hard life on the farm had disguised. Perhaps rural desolation was less intense than the desolation of the country club belt. Perhaps it was just the same. In his epic *USA* (1938) John Dos Passos makes it clear that Henry Ford may have left the farm, but took the values of country life with him to Wayne County, Michigan. 'The precepts he'd learnt out of *McGuffey's Reader*, his prejudices and preconceptions he has preserved clean and unworn as fresh-printed bills in the safe in a bank.'

In American literature cars frequently appear as symbols of material success, but also as machines capable of producing sensations of power and control. For their drivers, loosely located in a world of uncertain values, the possession of a car is a gratifying experience. Sinclair Lewis describes it in *Dodsworth* (1929):

To-night he was particularly uplifted because he was driving his first car. And it was none of your old-fashioned 'gasoline buggies' . . . The engine bulked in front, under a proud hood over two feet long, and the steering column was not straight but rakishly tilted. The car was sporting and rather dangerous, and the lights were powerful affairs fed by acetylene gas. Sam sped on, with a feeling of power, of dominating the universe, at twelve dizzy miles an hour.

In his 'Ballad of Faith' William Carlos Williams wrote 'No dignity without chromium/No truth but a glossy finish . . .' Two spare lines that suggest the poignancy of new cars, a bitter-sweet sensation of universal experience. For some people, owning a new car is the nearest they will ever get to perfection in an otherwise flawed and soiled life. The journalist, Eric Larrabee, caught the mood perfectly in an article he wrote in *Industrial Design* magazine in 1955:

Stand at night, on a corner in a strange town, and watch the cars go by. What is there so poignant in this? A sense of private destinies, of each making his own choice, of being independent of everything but statistics. The car owners choose – or think they do – when to stop and start, where to go. The automobile offers a vista of escape: for the adolescent, from parental planning; for the Negro, from Jim Crow; and for others, from less formal restrictions on their freedom of movement. Thus they are liberated to the loneliness (and perplexity) of their independence, and thus travel on the highway at night acquires its own tones of adventure and sorrow.

This same sense was expressed with less implied tragedy by Chuck Berry:

Ridin' along in my automobile,
My baby beside me at the wheel,

4

I stole a kiss at the turn of a mile,
My curiosity running wild –
Cruisin' and playin' the radio,
With no particular place to go

Cars have often been important motifs in American
cinema, touchstones of the *Zeitgeist*. In John Ford's *Grapes
of Wrath* (1940) and in his *Tobacco Road* (1941), the car is
shown as an innocent tool, an instrument of reconciliation
and a symbol of social well-being. But by the middle
fifties, when Eric Larrabee was writing, a decade of
unplanned post-war consumerism has changed the public
mood and cars begin not only to be criticized by
journalists, but also appear in the movies as pessimistic
motifs. At exactly the moment when US automobile
production was reaching its peak, Fritz Lang made *The
Big Heat* (1953), a movie where the breaker's yard is used
to create a tragic and menacing mood. By the early sixties,
with the growth of consumerism, in movies such as Elia
Kazan's *Splendour in the Grass* (1961) cars are beginning to
be seen as actually threatening the natural rhythms of
human life. By the time *The Car* was released in 1977 the
process was complete. The car that was once a liberation
was now hostile.

European attitudes to the car have been altogether
more courtly. Perhaps because the car was never quite so
necessary in Europe (where, states being smaller and
distances being shorter, public transport is more effective), it has been treated neither with such exaggerated
respect nor with such shocked repugnance as in North
America. Nonetheless, the potential of the car as both a
means and a symbol of freedom influenced European
artists, as well as American citizens. The dimensions of
the world had been changing since the 1880s when the
supply of electricity meant that, for the first time in
history, the source of power could be remote from its point

In the early movies the automobile often featured
as a symbol of optimism and prosperity, of the
American Dream on the move. By the fifties the
mood had changed and the car appears as a
memento mori, as in the elegiac breaker's yard scene
in Fritz Lang's *The Big Heat* (1953). By the
seventies, with severe urban congestion and some
pressing environmental problems, popular culture
began treating some cars as tokens of menace. In
The Car (1977) an anonymous, though highly
evocative, driverless automobile terrorizes
America: the Futurist dream became a nightmare
when machines developed minds of their own.

of application. Thirteen years later, radio telegraphy meant instant mobility of information and by the time Carl Benz's first automobile was perfected in 1886, the private individual was given his own means of escape. The critic, John Berger, once even suggested that the entire development of Cubism was an artistic response to this fragmentation of experience brought about by technology.

It is scarcely surprising that so emotive a machine as the liberating automobile has stimulated hyperbole. In Europe, always some way behind America in terms of prosperity, the car remained an important symbol longer. The Parisian savant, Roland Barthes (who met a poetic death under the wheels of a laundry truck) caught the mood exactly in his heroic (if ironic) comparison of the modern car with the medieval cathedral:

I think that cars today are almost the exact equivalent of the great gothic cathedrals; I mean the supreme creation of an era, conceived with passion by unknown artists, and consumed in image if not in usage by a whole population which appropriates them as a purely magical object . . .

Yet, despite its darker side, first seen and described by Ilya Ehrenburg in *The Life of the Automobile* (1929) and echoed by environmentalists and conspiracy theorists ever since, the allure of cars is indestructible. The freedom and the beauty and the power of a well-wrought machine evidently touches a universally sensitive part of the human soul.

Perhaps the single most significant aspect of man's relationship with his car is the element of power. Henry Kissinger once said, to an unfortunate journalist who had asked him what he saw in his job, 'Power is the greatest aphrodisiac'. A fast car has reserves of power. The very suggestion of power has in itself a strong erotic content. Designers, stylists, the creative people in advertising agencies, marketing men, all find their various ways of

7

expressing that power in the appearance of cars and in the software that surrounds their promotion and their sales. It can be mechanical power or fiscal power. It doesn't matter, but the state of the world proves that people find it arousing and attractive.

Just look at Guernsey. This tiny island, where the speed of motor cars is limited to 35 mph, probably has more Porsches per capita than anywhere else in the UK. They can never be driven at a fraction of the dynamic potential which engineers have struggled to build into them. These powerful cars are not transport, they are aphrodisiacs. They are sold as costumes and worn for sexual display. What follows attempts to explain some reasons why.

2 SYMBOLISM
The Golden Age of Gorp

General Motors' chief designer, Harley Earl, stands in the Arizona desert by one of his bizarre creations. The mid-fifties were America's most confident age, and Earl supplied the fantasy symbols for it. Incredibly, no one in senior management ever questioned the validity of the world's largest industrial undertaking goofing around with turbine cars got up to look like air force fighters. Earl wanted people to park illustrations from *Popular Mechanics* in their yards.

People need symbols. America depends on them. Someone once remarked that never since the high days of Byzantium has a civilization depended so thoroughly on these coded tokens. The size and scale of America and the rootless, shifting nature of its population required talismans so that individuals could advertise their allegiance to national values. A great many of these national values were, at least in the recent past, dictated by the motor industry. If the effects of symbolism could be measured in avoirdupois it is likely that the symbolism coming out of Detroit would have weighed as much as the sheet metal.

If American people needed symbolism, they got it from the motor industry and the interesting thing is that they got different sorts of symbolism each year. A marketing technique which ingeniously wedded the seductive power of symbols to the exigencies of capitalist mass-production was invented by a barnstorming Californian called Harley Earl, who went to work for General Motors and started their design department. The chief creative influences on Earl were his onetime Hollywood neighbour, Cecil B. de Mille, and Al Jolson, who he said taught him how to judge an audience. Earl's department was actually called 'Art and Color'. In a blacked-out ideas room he called the hatchery, Earl one day invented what he called 'the dynamic economy'. Other people called it planned obsolescence.

There are two views you can take of planned obsolescence. The canonical version of the first was Willy Loman's. In his play *Death of a Salesman*, Miller makes the wretched anti-hero say:

9

Once in my life I would like to own something outright before it's broken! I'm always in a race with the junkyard! Loman was upset about his washing machine, but it might just as well have been his car. The fact that in the forty years after the First World War American industry had used up more of the earth's resources than all of civilization in the preceding four thousand years produced reactions from other socially sensitive commentators, besides Arthur Miller.

One of them was Vance Packard, the man who was to consumerism what Marie Stopes was to unplanned parenthood. By 1960, when his book *The Waste Makers* was published, Packard had already written a lot of books and articles which looked at American achievements from a point of view which might most charitably be called sideways. Packard knew that since Alfred P. Sloan had written a General Motors internal memorandum in the early twenties, calling attention to his idea that *appearance* could actually be used as a sales tool, the automobile industry had become locked into a hectic race to excite the consumer by styling cars.

The thing was, that with Henry Ford's dedication to continuously refining his mass-production techniques so that the price of the Model 'T' had dropped to a mere $290, the profit margins had disappeared. Margins are what fascinate businessmen. Symbols are what fascinate consumers and with Harley Earl's invention of styling on Sloan's behalf, General Motors had, by the late 1920s, cars which could compete with Ford in terms of appearance, if not price. Almost simultaneously, a technical innovation occurred which gave Harley Earl another card to play: the Du Pont chemical company (an early major stockholder in General Motors) developed 'Duco' synthetic paint. Cars no longer needed to be Henry Ford's black. Detroit – released from its chromatic limitations –

entered a phase when strange contortions of the imagination were to take place in the service of industry.

Although many notable styling developments were made in the 1930s, the whole business only really took off after the Second World War when, during the 1950s, America had its Golden Age, when it seemed that indefinite economic growth was a realistic goal. The new inter-state freeways appeared during these Eisenhower years to reinforce the abstract economic vision with tangible evidence that it was possible to travel to infinity.

It is no surprise that in 1955, at the peak of the freeway boom, American car production reached its peak. Harley Earl had become Vice-President Styling of General Motors. Symbolism was at its most powerful.

Earl was more a wizard of kitsch than an engineer, an entrepreneur of ideas that were dramatic in their startling vulgarity. As a stylist, he didn't bother to draw much. Witnesses recall that he used to sprawl around in a Mies van der Rohe 'Barcelona' chair, pointing out details on flip charts with the toes of his handmade English shoes. Although he died in 1969, colourful stories about Earl are still doing the rounds of the international motor industry.

He used to call his beloved plating chro-n-ium and he could not pronounce aluminium without adding a number of syllables (which hardly mattered as he rarely used the stuff). Anatole Lapine, the man now in charge of the austerely technical Porsche Studio at Weissach in Germany, learnt his stuff in what (with more-or-less conscious reference to Nathanael West) he calls the University of Hard Knocks and, somewhat later, at the end of the toe of Harley Earl. Lapine describes the atmosphere in General Motors' design studios circa 1956:

The assignment at General Motors for an executive in charge of the Styling Division consisted in being responsible for five million General Motors cars getting sold annually. The method you elect . . . is yours! If you do not handle the job – if there are less than five million sold – your telephone will ring at midnight.

The task of the symbolism business was to adapt General Motors' technically banal chassis and its muscular engines to the requirements of American popular fantasies. The theatrical influences of deMille and Jolson helped Earl in this respect and so did something else he brought from Hollywood: sculptor's modelling clay. The use of clay instead of wood encouraged Earl's stylists and model-makers to create flowing, complex curves. Concept sketches were translated into three dimensional sculpture which became the medium through which the styling concept evolved. Drawings were subsidiary to this hands-on modelling process. Linesdraft drawings would be made and updated to record how work was progressing, but the actual appearance of, say, your Chevrolet Bel-Air was determined by development and analysis of a clay model.

This was the time when Earl, who was a physical giant, would terrify everybody in the studio, sometimes with his shoes, but sometimes with his metallic blue dinosaur stare. By criticism, recommendation and pointing with his shoes, Earl got what he wanted. At the end of a meeting he would ask if anybody disagreed with him . . . because if they did he wanted the sonofabitch to stand up and be identified. The full-size, earthy barges emerging from this primordial creative process were then translated into high-finish fibreglass for top management's approval. At the Motoramas which had taken the place of Alfred Sloan's legendary business lunches at the Waldorf-Astoria Hotel, Earl would reveal these 'dream' cars. These Motoramas were no wimpish presentations of a cautious new product, they were balls-out theatrical spectacles with dancing girls and live music. Excitement was considered a higher goal than information or science.

But what was the source of the imagery and symbolism with which Earl invested these designs? He was obsessed both with motor racing and with military aviation. For Earl, science was best if it could be kept strictly symbolic: he used to make fellow passengers on aeroplanes feel uncomfortable when he tore pages out of in-flight magazines if they contained pictures of aircraft he liked. He loved the *look* of planes, and in his dream cars he aimed to give the same impression of speed which fighters had when parked on the flight line. General Motors owned Allison, the aircraft engine company, so Earl had had an invitation to Selfridge Air Force Base during the middle of the Second World War where he saw Lockheed's new P-38, the pursuit plane with dramatic twin-tail booms, designed by that other maestro of techno-symbolism, Clarence 'Kelley' Johnson.

Earl loved the twin-tail booms as much as Luftwaffe pilots learned to fear them: the Germans called the P-38 the Zweiheckteufel. (With less colourful imagery the RAF proposed to call it the Lockheed 'Liverpool', but settled instead for the marginally more exciting 'Lightning'.) Earl settled for the booms: in 1948 they appeared as vestigial tail fins on the Cadillac Sedanet and eventually spread right through the General Motors product line.

Similarly, Earl's own first post-war dream car was called 'Le Sabre', after the F-86 jet which had taken his fancy. Its wraparound windshield (which virtually defied the production capabilities of Libbey–Owens–Ford, the Ohio glass company) was demanded by Earl because he thought it looked like the canopy of the military jet. The car, which Earl used for driving to his Grosse Pointe country club, as well as to frighten simple people enjoying street life, sported an extraordinary repertoire of ducts, scoops, vents, louvres and nozzles which, while all fake, realistically projected some of his fantasies about flight. Sigmund Freud would have added that they also projected his fascination with orifices. Later, it was used by Eisenhower when he ran NATO in Paris.

The symbols which Earl evolved in his personal dream cars were used sparingly, although inevitably, on General Motors' production cars. Starting with the high line models, rather than the proletarian ones, the public hungrily accepted them as details which conferred status on the owner. The Chevrolet Corvette grew right out of this process: it was the first dream car to reach production. It was America's only post-war sports car and the first 'personal' car, the forerunner of those special products created for what consultants nowadays call 'niche marketing'.

The Corvette was an American version of a sports car, like a hamburger is an American version of *filet mignon*. In the early 1950s Jaguar and MG alone had about one per cent of the American market and, if they were not flooding it, they were inundating the imaginations of the generation whose survival in a free world of consumerist fantasy gave rise to the post-war Baby Boom.

The Corvette appeared in 1953, named after a military vessel. As a vehicle for going around corners it was no use at all. The tyres were like the ones on medium-weight delivery trucks and its crude suspension made it pitch, roll and yaw like a raft in a heavy swell. Its handling and traction were similar in dynamic quality to a school bus. But it was an exquisite expression of the Earl styling philosophy: a ton of symbolism, good enough to eat. Many people's loins still tingle when they see a Corvette: the American mating rituals dutifully recorded in Coca-Cola advertisements throughout the fifties frequently show a Corvette chaperoning couples whose Levis are feeling the strain.

The 1956 Chevrolet Corvette. If young adult
libido were expressed in terms of metal, plastic
and plating it would look like this. Despite its
visual drama, the Corvette's crude engineering
made it more suitable for the drive-in than for
driving.

The brief to his terrified team of stylists was 'Go all the way and then back off', an instruction which they ignored perhaps because of its obvious sexual suggestiveness. They went all the way and then some. The dud six-cylinder was evocatively called 'Blue Flame'. The body shape, derived not only from aircraft, but also, in this case, loosely based on coachbuilt Ferraris and things Earl had seen on his annual tour of the European motor shows had sensuous lines and striking details. Starbursts of evocation dribbled out of its scalloped side panels. Its lavish, nipped and tucked interior, with glistening Naugahyde up-holstery screamed sun, sex and speed. It was a car for the drive-in, rather than driving.

Ford tried it too. In the mid-fifties America's Ford Motor Company decided it needed a new product and it put all its resources behind one. The new product was the Edsel and, before the launch of New Coke in 1985, it became the greatest marketing disaster in modern history.

Its designer was Roy A. Brown, Junior, whose career had begun at General Motors and developed via American Airlines and the Piper aeroplane company, before he joined Ford in 1953. His first job had been the Lincoln 'Futura' dream car (which eventually became the Batmobile).

Under Harley Earl, General Motors' cars had already become longer and lower, and everyone was aping the General's lead. While Chrysler was working on what it modestly called the 'Hundred Million Dollar Look', the emphasis on all mid-fifties American cars was overwhelmingly *horizontal*. They looked like vast, melted briquettes of Neapolitan ice cream with gaping chrome jaws and chrome dib-dabs.

Such was the appetite for novelty excited by Earl's concept of designed-in obsolescence that when Bob Jones, one of Brown's colleagues, pointed out that cars used to have vertical grilles, it was greeted as an important revelation. To allay fears that the Edsel's vertical grille might suggest a return to rational engineering (as the radiators themselves were, as ever, still upright), Jones assured his leader that 'It can be designed to look new and disfunctional'. According to C. Gayle Warnock, head of PR for the Edsel:

Their goal was to design a car that would look like a leader in its price field, suggest top performance and meet the psychological needs of the motoring public.

They worked in conditions of obsessive secrecy: three different passes were required for entry into the Design Center. (What does this secrecy *mean*?) At the presentation to Ford Senior Staff Brown explained:

The front theme of this newest car combines nostalgia with modern straightforward vertical thrust, while the side to rear unification creates a novel feeling of harmonious relationship and apparent increase in length from a three-quarter rear view.

The grille was the most significant part of an American car's design, because as Eugene Jaderquist of *Motor Life* pointed out:

We have been conditioned to accept the grille as the single true identifying feature of the automobile.

Critics who liked the Edsel compared the grille with auspicious precedents in automobile history, the La Salle and Alfa-Romeos. Art Baum, a staff writer on the *Saturday Evening Post*, got near the real meaning when he said of the grille:

I may see it as a classic eleventh-century Norman shield; you may see it as a horse collar . . .

a comment that inevitably calls to mind one of the more imaginative, if crude, similes used by Mordecai Richler,

Before Coca-Cola changed the taste of Coke in 1985, Ford's Edsel was the biggest blunder by a major American corporation. The result of meticulous product-planning directed at creating an automobile package to satisfy the consumers' dreams, the Edsel flopped. Named after one of his under-achieving sons, the Edsel betrayed the sentimental streak in Henry Ford (he had named the Ford Fairlane after his maternal grandmother's home in Cork). Struggling to understand the reasons for the commercial disaster, Ford's PR team discovered that some customers found the Edsel's vertical grille uncomfortably similar to a vagina.

when he said one of his novel's heroines had '. . . a cunt like a horse's collar . . .' I do not know whether the *Saturday Evening Post* staff writer and Mordecai Richler share an interest in the psychology of Jung, but the common ground of their very different observations suggests something about the universal appeal of symbols.

But a lawyer from Fargo, North Dakota, got straight to the point when he wrote to Ford's PR staff (who, in their defence, described him as 'sexually sick') that:

It was bad enough that Studebaker saw fit to design a car whose front reminds me of male testicles, but now you have gone that company one better by designing a car with a front like a female vagina.

The fact was that the grille of the Ford Edsel looked like a fanny, although it is hard to see how this morpho-erotic effect could have contributed to the car's failure in the market-place, when the Jaguar 'E' type's success was widely attributed by psychologists to the very similarity its profile had to the male organ.

According to Uwe Bahnsen, Ford of Europe's present head of design, the Edsel failed because:

It was hitting a market that was totally opposed to that sort of car. If the car could have been produced when the information they used was gathered, it probably could have been a reasonably successful car, but the implementation period was so long . . . the market had changed. The main problem with the Edsel was that nobody, at any time in the programme, took their vision beyond yesterday and today. Every input into the project stopped with today. There was no projection and this made it hopelessly outdated by the time it arrived on the market.

Cars are loaded with symbolism both overt and covert, something which afforded Dada artist Francis Picabia a great many effective opportunities in image-making. According to Maurizio Fagiolo, his love of cars was

The feline Jaguar 'E' type went on sale in 1961, a
direct descendant of the 'D' type which last won
the Le Mans 24-hour race in 1957. The tense,
smooth, sculpted bodywork looks fast even when
the car is stationary. The aggressive stance,
together with the bulbous shape and the particular
treatment of the radiator air intake provided a
substantial basis for critics to describe the Jaguar
as a phallic symbol.

'mythical'. One page of his widow Olga Mohler's monograph has Picabia posing with some of his automobile lovers: a 1922 Delage is labelled 'une passion!' Another shows him static, but in the driving seat, with his head thrust back with a stationary *frisson* of incarnate pride. In *L'Anneau de Saturne* (1970) Germaine Everling says that Picabia had an almost physical relationship with his cars, lost in admiration of the details, thrilled to pat their ungiving coachwork. He thought his American Mercer, delivered in 1919, was 'the most beautiful car you can see'. Present day admirers of Porsche sports cars frequently use the term 'hard' as an approbation of the vehicle's quality: its sexual connotations are lost on only a few listeners . . .

In his art, Picabia was no less forthright about the erotic content of cars. In 1917 with ink and metallic gouache, he meticulously drew an internal combustion valve, its spring and its guide. He called it 'Flamenca' and made no comment. But mute it was more eloquent still: the reciprocating valve resembles in its action the rhythms of sex, the valve itself the penis, the guide the female sheath. The spring stands for goodness knows what, but perhaps Picabia saw its natural tendency to return to normality as a mechanical metaphor of the ultimate median produced by the successive thrills and depressions of sex.

A painting of 1919, *L'Enfant Carburateur*, shows Picabia demonstrating the erotic potential of cars and their components to the full. Based on a technical drawing of a Claudel carburettor (rather as he had once before based a drawing on a Delco wiring diagram), Picabia's *Enfant* is a *tour de force* of mechanical symbolism. Like the valve, parts of the carburettor suggest sex, in a rather vague way. Curious inscriptions on the picture at once enhance and confuse the effect: 'Waltz in Jacket', 'Dissolution of Prolongation', 'Crocodile Method'. According to William Canfield, in his book *Picabia, His Art, Life and Times*, they

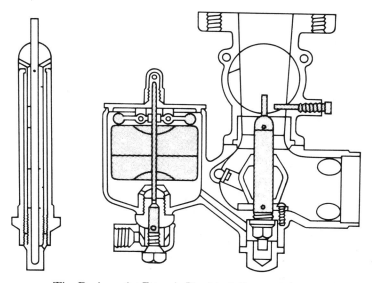

The Dada artist Francis Picabia (1879–1953) was
fascinated by machines, and by motor cars in
particular. To their component parts he attached
a special significance. By artful juxtapositions of
image and word in his paintings and collages
Picabia created an erotic language out of the
illustrations from workshop manuals. The Claudel
carburettor featured in his mysterious painting,
L'Enfant Carburateur.

are suggestive of tensions in his private life during a year when both his wife and his mistress were carrying his child. Certainly, they are indications that Picabia saw in cars more than mere transport. Like his friend, Marcel Duchamp, who used the expression 'love gasoline' to describe the fluid which drove the 'motor' in his own erotic parable, *The Large Glass*, Picabia used mechanical imagery as an embodiment and as a reflection of human passions.

The same sentiment occurred in America. In his 1926 poem 'XIX', e.e. cummings describes running in a new car as similar to making love with a virgin:

she being Brand

-new;and you
know consequently a
little stiff i was
careful of her and (having

thoroughly oiled the universal
joint tested my gas felt of
her radiator made sure her springs were O.

K.)i went right to it flooded-the-carburetor cranked her

up, slipped the
clutch(and then somehow got into reverse she
kicked what
the hell)next
minute i was back in neutral tried and

again slo-wly; bare,ly nudg. ing(my

lev-er Right-
oh and her gears being in
A 1 shape passed
from low through
second-in-to-high like
greasedlightning)just as we turned the corner of Divinity

avenue i touched the accelerator and give

her the juice, good
                              (it
was the first ride and believe i we was
happy to see how nice she acted right up to
the last minute coming back down by the Public
Gardens i slammed on
the

internalexpanding
&
externalcontracting
brakes Bothatonce and

brought allof her tremB
-ling
to a: dead.

stand-
;Still)

     Perhaps the greatest marketing coup of the twentieth
century was to relate the automobile to sex, an endeavour
amply aided by artists and writers who eagerly seized
upon the car's liberating power as a potent symbol in an
age which disdained religion. The sexual symbolism of the
automobile emerged as a self-conscious marketing tool
during the period which witnessed the refinement of mass-
production. Indeed, there is a sense in which this
symbolism and mass-production are inseparable. Karl
Marx wrote:

Nature builds no machines . . . These are products of
human will over nature . . . They are the organs of human
brains . . . the power of knowledge objectified.

It is the car's power and its inherent conquest of natural
limitations that lie at the root of its erotic appeal. Henry
Ford added:

Design will take more advantage of the power of the
machine to go beyond what the hand can do and will give
us a whole new art.

25

To Ford, the car was a liberating force, but he was less explicit about the attractions of its *power*. Karl Ludvigsen wrote that man has 'an almost destructive obsession for physical might' and cars have provided expressions of this will to power. By multiplying human forces cars become machines for creating supermen. The contrast between the inherent docility of the machine and the forces it is capable of generating emphasize the stimulating character of the man/machine relationship. It is quasi-erotic: the hint of violence is familiar stuff to the pornographer because power, of course, suggests control. The capacity for control promises gratification. Taken to the ultimate, this becomes perverse.

When cars appear in pop culture the ever-present motif is of status and power: driving in traffic as a form of sexual display. A curiously powerful expression of the erotic suggestiveness of the automobile is science fiction writer J.G. Ballard's book *Crash!* (1973), which he describes as the first pornographic novel inspired by technology:

Do we see in the car crash, a sinister portent of a nightmare marriage between sex and technology?

In *Crash!* the car is a sexual motif: the narrator says, 'I could bring myself to orgasm simply by thinking of the car in which we performed our sexual acts.' And later, a short passage suggests that the tactile qualities of the car are as stimulating as female flesh:

His hand was raised at right-angles to his forearm, measuring out the geometry of the chromium roof-sill, while his right hand moved down the girl's thighs . . .

In this robust context the narrative serves as little more than pretext for indulgent fantasies about new sexual patterns established in the nightmare world of car crash victims. In the tangled wreck all conventions of modesty and self-control collapse and are replaced by a perverse new logic: with bodies thrown into indecent postures, a young woman urinates involuntarily, her crotch stained with blood. Ballard writes of the 'mysterious eroticism of wounds' but more tellingly still of the 'perverse logic of blood-soaked instrument panels'. He creates a world of erotic values where only crash victims, with their maimed bodies, can understand and enjoy the rules of this new erotic game where the undisciplined release of sexual tension can reveal unlimited opportunities for gratification:

I dreamed of other accidents that might enlarge this repertory of orifices.

Popular literature frequently treats the car as a sexual symbol. Stephen King specializes in a genre which combines cleverly detailed descriptions of small-town America which give off a very strong sense of place, admixed with ham-fisted, although energetic, episodes about demonic possession. In *Christine* (1983) King sets up his story with Dennis as narrator in a *Catcher in the Rye* style. Dennis's best friend is Arnie, a boy with a quirky sense of humour and zits. Life in Libertyville is a pleasant, if banal, progress of parental and sibling squabbles, mild restraint, laughable teachers and adorable girls. This background helps lull the reader into a sense of rightness and comfort and security which is, of course, exploded as the story develops.

A flawed hero, Arnie falls in love with Christine . . . but Christine is not a lissom high school kid, Christine's a car. In this case, a blood red Plymouth Fury, whose 1956 predecessor introduced the American public to the thrilling experience of speed in a domestic product: the first versions were painted white with gold anodized appliqué body mouldings. The 303 cubic inch V8, with its solid lifters, competition valve springs, dual exhausts and carter

In his book *Christine* (1983), virtuoso horror novel
author Stephen King gave diabolic personality to
a 1957 Plymouth Fury. Beneath the bravura
narrative there lies a substantial truth about
drivers' relationships with their cars: sexual and
demonic possession compete for supremacy. It is a
case of possess, or be possessed.

four-barrel carburettor producing 240 brake horse power, had one production car reaching 145 mph on the Daytona Beach track in Florida. Even the briefest technical description of this car is titillating: the specification is like a protracted crescendo which will eventually erupt into an explosive celebration of speed. Metaphors of love and marriage occur in every description of Arnie's car.

It is always female: 'If the car won't start, curse it and be sure you curse it female.'

Arnie's first act of possession is to *buy* the car, in a chapter whose title, 'Arnie Gets Married', displays a complex litter of meanings combining sex and money and ownership in a trilogy of intense eroticism. There is sexual jealousy too: 'Cars are girls' it says on page 234; 'her hard, cool surface' on page 393. The gender identification of the Plymouth is clear enough, but the subtext is even more interesting. Arnie's relationship with his Plymouth Fury is token not only of the sort of morpho-eroticism which cars can stimulate, but is more significant still as evidence of all the suppressed anxieties which cars provoke and their designers and marketers exploit. The anxiety quotient becomes clearer as the supernatural elements in the homespun story begin to dominate the humdrum account of small-town life.

Christine is a woman and the horrors she visits on all who 'possess', or even 'ride' her reveals a strongly misogynist streak in the author . . . and, given the context of the book, we can take Stephen King to stand for Mr America. He is saying, as Christine develops healing properties (her cracked windshield mends itself), as Dennis dreams of her as a monster ('God, it's unending Fury'), as Christine stalls (when Arnie tells a new girlfriend he is in love with her), as the car goes automatic on an unmanned trip (and revenges herself with the death of three boys who once damaged her) and the pattern of supernatural destruction intensifies, that cars are a great deal more than they seem. In King's own words, the ownership of a car is 'a disturbing parody of the act of love'. And the embodiment of this act in literature is the car as a seductive woman with sinister powers. With their crude, but effective sculpture, aping the curves and orifices of the female form, Detroit designers had known this for more than thirty years.

3 SPEED
Romance with a Machine

The surest method of suggesting speed, even while cruising sedately on California boulevards, was to loot aerospace imagery. What on an airplane was hot, dirty and dangerous became sanitized in dream cars into crisp, seductive detail. The orifices speak for themselves.

Speed, Aldous Huxley once remarked, is the only entirely novel sensation of the twentieth century. Trains made speed a democratic experience and a century and a half later, the refined technology of jet travel took away the sensation. The private car made this extraordinary experience *personal* . . .

It is one of the great achievements of twentieth-century marketing to have forged an equation, even an identity, between speed and success: the basis for it is, perhaps, indicated by Stirling Moss's remark that 'There are two things no man will admit he can't do well . . . drive and make love.'

Adapted to the gewgaws of consumerism, the crucial relationship between sex and speed has been a powerful tool in marketing. When Audi-Volkswagen did market research among those buyers who regularly spend £25,000 on a new car, they found that 23 out of the 40 they interviewed *still* spoke about Jaguar at Le Mans, where the marque won five brave victories in the famous endurance race, but more than thirty years ago!

A fast car demonstrates professional success and suggests sexual prowess, but how did this curious link between speed on the tarmac and tingling in the loins come about? Sigmund Freud's 1905 essay on infantile sexuality gives us a clue:

We must also mention the production of sexual excitation by rhythmic mechanical agitation of the body . . . The existence of these pleasurable sensations . . . is confirmed by the fact that children are so fond of games of passive movement, such as swinging and being thrown up into the

air, and insist on such games being incessantly repeated
. . . The shaking produced by driving in carriages and
later by railway travel exercises such a fascinating effect
upon older children that every boy . . . has at one time or
other in his life wanted to be an engine driver . . . It is a
puzzling fact that boys take such an extraordinarily
intense interest in things connected with railways and, at
the age at which the production of fantasies is most active
(shortly before puberty), use those things as the nucleus of
a symbolism that is peculiarly sexual. A compulsive link of
this kind between railway travel and sexuality is clearly
derived from the pleasurable character of the sensations of
movement . . . The combination of fright and mechanical
agitation produces the severe hysteriform, traumatic
neurosis . . . these influences, which, when they are of
small intensity, become sources of sexual excitation, lead
to a profound disorder in the sexual mechanism or
chemistry if they operate with exaggerated force.

Severe acceleration can lead to a complete loss of vision
(black-out), or restricted vision (grey-out). Leading up to
that, heart rate always increases under positive g and
researchers have found that racing drivers' pulses are
frequently in the 160 to 180 range. Under acceleration, as
blood pools in the legs, less is actually delivered to the
heart, hence there is a fall in cardiac output and, what
with one thing and another, you feel *high*.

In terms of *associations*, driving cars fast is an act of
recklessness which, perhaps, recaptures some elements of
the thrill of adolescent sex. The people, usually men, who
buy fast cars are often of years sufficiently mature for the
exciting, frantic couplings of youth to be only a memory.
With sex a safe, familiar component of married life, like
going to the supermarket or stacking the dishwasher, a fast
car (at least potentially) offers a landscape of thrill which in
other respects the years have washed away. Similarly
women who drive ostentatiously fast cars, seem to be
making a statement at once titillating and de-masculating:

rather like a strange, attractive woman flaunting her availability, but making it clear that you are not included. A female executive at Wight Collins Rutherford Scott, the London advertising agency that handles BMW advertising confirmed that it is considered by her male colleagues to be an overt sexual statement for a woman to drive any BMW more powerful than the base model in each series.

There is something specially and *directly* arousing about the experience of speed, too, whether it suggest the risks associated with being committed to extremes or, as Freud supposed, it has some sort of direct action on our nervous systems. There are people whose greatest thrill is taking off in an airliner. Here, the acceleration experienced is $\frac{1}{4}$ g. In a Formula One racing car it is altogether different. In his book *At Speed*, Karl Ludvigsen describes the thrill of driving a racing car:

For one who enjoys motor-racing there is no satisfaction that surpasses that of a perfect sweep through a difficult turn, a rapid-fire tattoo of gear changes, the strain in the neck muscles against hard acceleration. These are joys that the racing driver shares with no one because he cannot. They can only be experienced.

There may be endocrinological aspects of this solitary experience, which seems, to the dispassionate observer, at least somewhat onanistic. But while other forms of masturbation have proved a rich source of inspiration for literature, what Fangio and others discovered on the racing circuits of the world, culture has struggled to accommodate. To some of the most influential artists of the twentieth century, the racing car has been an ideal. An expression in engineering of effects they struggled, often unsuccessfully, to create in the more prosaic media of oil-on-canvas, marble or film. A generation seduced by the romance of the machine found itself lost in awe at the urgent beauty of these exciting, dynamic theorems in metal. Lartigue captured them in photographs, Marinetti projected the mood in his ranting propaganda. No one really caught it in literature.

Enzo Ferrari had wanted to write: his first public 'appearance' was a by-line, at the age of sixteen, in the *Gazzetta dello Sport* and he reminisced:

My youth had known three dominant passions, three great dreams: operetta tenor, sport journalist, racing driver.

Later he explained the circumstances of the racing driver:

Between man and machine there exists a perfect equation: fifty per cent machine and fifty per cent man.

This equation clearly suggests that the idea of mechanical intercourse, that parody of the act of love, lies only a little beneath the surface of people who are fascinated by fast cars. Freud's essay on Infantile Sexuality, with its discussion of the effects of motion, was published in the same volume as his essay about the erotic potential of mechanical forms.

The Futurist poet and pamphleteer, Marinetti, found that the sound of a racing car was more moving than the sight of classical sculpture in the Louvre. The French painter, Fernand Léger, exalted machines to such a degree that he made a film called *Le Ballet mécanique* whose stars were the engines of Bugatti racing cars. It was said that Ettore Bugatti himself so prized the aesthetic value of his engineering work that he made wooden models of his engines, like a sculptor's *bozzetti,* so that he could assess their formal beauty before committing the design to the engineering shop. In Le Corbusier's *Vers une Architecture* the best cars of the day are compared to the buildings of Periclean Athens. One of his favourite photographs shows him, flat cap reversed, sitting in the cockpit of a beautiful little Alfa-Romeo on the Monza race track, just outside Milan.

34

To the painters, architects and designers of the
Modern Movement, the machine was a metaphor
of contemporary values. The perfect geometry of
mechanical engineering was a paradigm in a
post-war world of economic depression still not
fully purged of Victorian fustian. French painter
Fernand Léger (1881–1955) made his abstract
film, *Le Ballet mécanique*, in 1923–24. Its subject
matter was gear trains and whirling pulleys.

The car designer Ettore Bugatti came from a
family of artists and sculptors. It was said that he
modelled engine components, including
crankshafts, in wood so that he could assess them
in aesthetic terms before committing them to
production. The engine of his Type 35 racing car
is almost the perfect Newtonian machine.

These fine credentials make the modern Grand Prix a perplexing experience for someone who knows about the history of the relationship between the modern imagination and the fast car. At a Grand Prix the atmosphere is tantalizing and the cars always excite, but the environment and its population is always a disappointment. The days are past when racing drivers had freckled arms, Fred Perry shirts and every hand-hammered car had a Jubilee clip. Gone are the Italian racing drivers with names like diseases: Tarufi, Varzi, Nuvolari. The modern racing driver is self-obsessed, preening, spoilt and very rich.

Enzo Ferrari disdains them. He never uses planes to follow the international Grands Prix. He scarcely leaves Modena, observing modern motor-racing either from his immensely solemn drawing room or from the restaurant Il Cavallino hard by his factory. If you think about what he looks like you can almost summon the smell of furniture polish, a vision of the bowl of fruit and the low frequency buzz of afternoon sun in Emiglia. There was a primitive competitive ideal that obsessed Enzo Ferrari and it was nothing to do with getting Tracey's knickers off before half past ten, Radio Horizon 102.5 FM, Laser 558 Radio, nasty cigarettes, anoraks, keg beer, jeans, crisps, training shoes, Cortinas with whip aerials, artificial ice cream, bikini briefs or any of the other philistine detritus you find at, say, Brands Hatch. Enzo Ferrari could not even imagine it, but you know that if someone described it to him he would hate it. The British Grand Prix is as if all the cultural values of a Bromley discothèque were suddenly admixed with a trillion pounds of international public relations and thrown up all over the suburban Kent countryside.

Yet somewhere in this Gomorrah of sponsored nastiness there remain superb, beautiful racing cars and their fascinating designers. Although the Paddock on race day

The 1986 Grand Prix Ferrari.

looks like the set of a low-budget Vietnam movie, with lots of Ray-Bans, elephant's intestines of television cable, important people with clipboards, bad roads, an atmosphere of menace and a smell of pee, there are treasures to be found. The huge trailers used by the racing teams are like mobile temples where the values of their sponsors are worshipped.

The British Williams team has a magnificent Leyland T45 and in it no one moves. Goodyear has an American motorhome where they serve you German chocolate biscuits and international instant coffee. It has K-Mart décor. The Techniques d'Avant-Garde trailer is like the Space Shuttle adapted for use on the motorways of Europe.

Only Ferrari's trailer has the power to move the spirit. Its one whimsical detail is the pack of *amaretti* on the driver's side of the IVECO tractor. All else is solemn, gloomy beauty. Infinitely sad Latin mechanics handle the most lovingly built of all racing cars, probably wishing they were in Enzo Ferrari's drawing room. The star driver, a young Milanese called Michele Alboreto, chats to his wife. It is pretentious, but it's hard not to bring to mind the strutting, trilling pride of Musetta in Puccini's *La Bohème* as you see him talk to his wife while the mechanics tinker with his car. What does he think, minutes later, as he hustles, barks, rasps and wriggles the difficult, dangerous, beautiful car around a circuit designed for warmed-over Ford Anglias?

No other racing driver looks as tragic as Michele Alboreto, although plenty have a lot to be worried about. They live in a terrible world, mitigated only by the possibility of glory and kept sharp only by the prospect of violent death. Near the elegant Alboreto you can hear people boast about having spent Christmas in Hawaii with George Harrison. People riffle through executive briefcases with combination locks, looking for freebies. In the Press Box you can, if you want it, buy a pint of Harp lager at ten to ten. There are raffia waste paper baskets so scorched by John Player Specials that it looks as though someone has used them to snuff out the flame on an RB-211.

One man in the modern world of Grand Prix motor racing maintains a sense of the forces of destiny that control the great Enzo Ferrari. He is Gordon Murray, a South African engineer who designs the cars of the British Brabham team. Murray looks as though he just might, some time ago, actually have been to a discothèque in Bromley, but appearances can be deceptive, even if, in Murray's case, that appearance comprises: long hair, shades, a Walkman doing Siouxsie and the Banshees, a Rolling Stones T-shirt, Day-glo sneakers, gum, Davidoff cigarillos and a laid-back fuck-that air of someone who's been seeing it all for about a decade and a half. It is a disguise which camouflages his genuinely irreverent character: a conversation with Gordon Murray after a walk around Brands Hatch is like having your compass re-set after a nasty bout in a magnetic storm.

Murray has huge integrity, ideas of genuine vision and maintains a Zen-like calm, despite having ridden his Honda VF1000R two-wheeled missile all the way from Guildford to Kent. He likes the bike so much he says he could look at it all day. The severe, yet optimistic, motorbike presents a prospect altogether different from the here-today tinsel that will be gone-tomorrow in the world he inhabits. He will talk design principles.

You can ask him whether, in the interests of racing efficiency, he has ever had to do things which offended the good sense of a trained engineer. He says a sort of yes. Look at the winglets at the front of his latest Brabham. He says they are an affront to all known standards of 'virtue'

Gordon Murray, the South African engineer who
designs contemporary Brabham racing cars.
Murray is the most technologically fastidious
designer of his generation, reading *Aviation Week and
Space Technology* for his inspiration.

in engineering: 'No aerodynamicist could have designed them: he'd rather cut his hands off'. But if it makes the car go faster it gets the nod.

In Murray's world developments happen quickly: he's interested in the aerospace industry as a paradigm of the technical, but he finds progress there too slow. The beauty in designing racing cars is that it's like a high technology cottage industry: Murray uses a pocket calculator, not a CAD-CAM system. Using the facilities of his workshop he can employ a new material two weeks after reading about it in *Aviation Week and Space Technology*. Formula One, he says, is pure fantasy for the engineer. In designing a racing car, he can take it to the limit every time . . .

In a fast road car like a Porsche 911 you can replicate motor-racing, and take it nearly to the limit, even on the Gloucester Road. That's to say, even if you don't go fast. In fact, like making love, there are some theorists who argue that it's more fun if you do it slowly. Either way, it's a sensuous act.

With a Porsche, the stimulation of the senses begins with the car's appearance: it has what a Porsche designer calls 'the winning look which weapons have', a functional, purposeful air. Somewhat aggressive, but mitigated by sensitive details and the odd feminine radius. Like a ruched, go-faster, armour-plated turtle. Although the 911's ancestry from Volkswagen is very clear (their bodies were both inspired by the same man, Erwin Kommenda), the simultaneous suggestion of menace and restraint is a titillating combination which, as the marque's sales rise in every known territory, competitors have struggled to imitate.

Inside the car its acute lack of ergonomic efficiency is a demonstration that a higher experience is on offer than that available in, say, a Volvo. The contempt for one sort of function so as better to perform another is, for all the

The 1985 Porsche 962 sports-racing car. Even on
this most functional of machines there are elements
which are semantic rather than purely utilitarian.
According to the *Hauptabteilungsleiter* of Porsche's
Studio, American designer Anatole Lapine, they
embody 'the winning look that weapons have'.

world, like a woman wearing a tight leather skirt and precarious patent black stilettos: hobbling is erotic.

Inside the dark car, it is like a bunker. Of all the instruments, the only one visible is a clock. Anal-retentive Germans expect to time their arrival at *Autobahn Ausfahrts* to the minute and the super-reliability of their motor industry's products allows them to do so with precision.

On contact, the engine spins and thrashes. The gearchange is like a poor truck's: it baulks and grinds and snatches, then you penetrate the gate, foot down and you're away. Snatching changes seems rough, but as the transmission takes up the power, the tail squats very satisfyingly and you are slung forward so fast you want to stop. You do at the lights. The 500 yards to Beauchamp Place can be harrowing or it can be breathtaking. It is a hard car, but when you've parked, you want to do it again. Not for nothing is wrestling a woman to the ground a familiar motif in soft pornography.

4 CULTURE
Little Bastards

In material things the German cultural tradition depends on detail, refinement, and research, and the Porsche 911 is the embodiment of it. King's Road and Rodeo Drive boutique owners, more-or-less ignorant of *Geistesgeschichte*, swarm to buy this potent derivative of Ferdinand Porsche's original Volkswagen. The 911, which has been continuously improved for a quarter-century, is living proof that pedigree is bankable.

The car became the ultimate consumer durable, but before that it was the ultimate talisman of an age which worshipped the machine. In the car, visionary artists found a metaphor for the democratic potential of a new order, what Guillaume Apollinaire called 'l'esprit nouveau'. The history of nineteenth and early twentieth-century literature furnishes us with many examples of artists who sensed the aesthetic opportunities which pistons, crown wheels and beautiful coachwork offered.

But none was more articulate, one might almost say frenzied, than the Italian poet and pamphleteer Filippo Tommaso Marinetti, the founder of Futurism. In an article published in *Le Figaro* in 1909, Marinetti declared the need for a new art which embodied the realities of modern life. The article includes this bravura passage of sado-erotic kitsch (after a car crash):

O maternal ditch, almost full of muddy water! Fair factory drain! I gulped down your nourishing sludge; and I remembered the blessed black breast of my Sudanese nurse . . . When I came up – torn, filthy and stinking – from under the capsized car, I felt the white-hot iron of joy pass through my heart!

Marinetti projected his own enthusiasm for dynamism, movement and the implicit eroticism of power into a campaign for a new aesthetic:

We intend to exalt aggressive action, a feverish insomnia, the racer's stride, the mortal leap, the punch and the slap.

Thus, street sounds, racing cars, bombing raids, recipes calling for the inclusion of petrol, and acoustic poems

45

mimicking the sound of aero engines replaced the stable, classical and romantic forms of nineteenth-century art. His most famous remark is specially relevant in this context:

A racing car . . . is more beautiful than the Victory of Samothrace.

A pronouncement which the historian of Futurism, Marianne Martin, described as a 'climactic statement of the insistent role of the machine in modern art'.

Although Futurism was unquestionably an influence on the formulation of Mussolini's fascism (along with a ragbag of pacifist, anarchist, syndicalist and nationalist 'theories'), Marinetti and his artistic colleagues were ambivalent towards politics, a position reflected by Il Duce himself whose admiration for speed and noise was tempered by his suspicions that, because it predated his Fascism, Futurism must itself be tainted with the claustrophobic bourgeois past he repudiated.

Mussolini was a philistine towards the visual arts, but had a genuine love of grand opera. His contempt for Toscanini kept him away from La Scala for the first night of *Turandot* in 1926, but Il Duce decided to rabble-rouse the crowds gathered outside. His attitude to Puccini is not known, but it is certain that the composer loved machines. He was also fond of whores: his Lucchese contemporaries called him 'maestro cuccumeggiante' (the whores' composer). He raced a motor boat, made mechanical toys for his own amusement and posed for a surrealistic photograph with his head in a mangle, as if to extract new ideas. His passion for cars arose out of a passion for speed which he shared with the Futurists. Driving back from Lucca one night in February, 1903, with his chauffeur, Ultimo, Puccini's Clement crashed, holding up work on *Madame Butterfly* and leaving him with a permanent limp after a compound fracture of the right leg was improperly set.

Although his convalescence depressed him – 'Addio tutto, addio Butterfly, addio mia vita!' he melodramatically wrote – the incident did nothing to assuage his appetite for speed: next he bought faster cars, including a Rolls-Royce and an eight-cylinder Lancia. Studies of his operas have shown that Puccini's life is reflected in his work. The soaring climaxes, protracted crescendos and explosions of power recall not only a journey in his car, but also passages in his bed.

The German approach is different. The German passion is for *Forschung* (research), rather than display. Deriving from traditions beginning with Prussian militarism and receiving extra force from the superb national standards of technical education, it is, nonetheless, an obsessive and inward-looking form of self-love. *Forschung* is apparent everywhere: Europe's very first (and still best) wind tunnel was created at Stuttgart's Motor Vehicle Research Institute by Wunibald Kamm in 1930. Still today, Germans spend as much on Research and Development as the entire motor industries of France, Italy and the United Kingdom combined. For a company of its size, Porsche files a disproportionate number of patents, the surest evidence of active research.

Prussian military traditions have surely had an influence on recent and contemporary German industrial practice. Clausewitz, in his book *Grundsatze des Kriegführens*, makes use of extended metaphors which liken the army to a machine. He regrets that the human stuff of the army is not as reliable and as predictable as a machine. The sense is of a longing for man to attain the functional perfection of clockwork, or of internal combustion. The military theorist goes on to explain that war is an extension of politics by other means. In this context, it is not fanciful to misquote him: *Forschung* is the sexual act carried on by other means.

There is a 1934 photograph of a moustachioed man,

The 1936 Auto-Union Grand Prix car, designed
by Ferdinand Porsche. Following Hitler's speech
at the 1933 Berlin Motor Show, racing cars
became elements of Nazi propaganda with
state-financed German technology blowing all the
competition into the weeds on the circuits of
Europe.

formal in his morning dress, explaining some aspects of his new Auto-Union racing car. The exchange is a little unbalanced: the man listening looks tense, the other relaxed and amused. It is a black and white picture, but you get the impression that our designer is blushing: his eyes are shut and his lips are slightly pursed, as if in embarrassment, or is it pride? The scene is the Chancellery in Berlin. The car designer is Ferdinand Porsche and the man he is talking to is Adolf Hitler. With them is racing driver Hans Stuck von Villiez together with Korpsführer Konrad Huehnlein, head of the NSKK (National Socialist Automobile Corps). Earlier that year Professor Porsche had been awarded 'Citizenship of the Reich' by Goebbels, the Nazi Propaganda Minister. Claiming disinterest in politics, the great engineer said 'I'm afraid there's nothing much we can do about it'.

Three years later the scene was repeated, and also photographed, at the Berlin Automobile Show. Now Professor Porsche looks more harrowed, Hitler more serious. Porsche is explaining the technicalities of his new 'people's car' to the Führer. Around them are Reichsleiter Dr Robert Ley, leader of the *Deutsche Arbeitsfront* and Dr Bodo Lafferentz, head of the *Kraft durch Freude* movement. *Kraft durch Freude* means Strength through Joy. Usually abbreviated to KdF, this slogan was the given name for the car we now know as the Volkswagen. The KdF-Wagen.

Hitler was a master of symbolism and the opportunities to use technology had not escaped him. Nazis preferred slogans to morals and *Kraft durch Freude* was coined at just about the same time as *Arbeit macht Frei* and . . . *Vorsprung durch Technik*. Curiously, a lot of the technical imperative driving Nazi Germany came from Ford. So, some say, did the financial imperative as well: it has been rumoured that Henry Ford bankrolled the Munich Beer

49

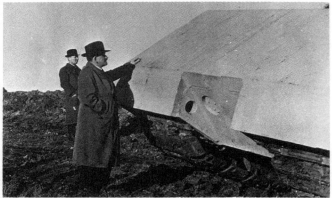

Ferdinand Porsche (1875–1951) had a
relationship with Hitler. Not only did the Führer
commission the great Austrian engineer to design
his 'people's car' (Volkswagen), but the Porsche
*Konstruktionsbüro für Motoren-Fahrzeug-Luftfahrzeug
und Wasserfahrzeugbau* also designed the Leopard
tank. In 1944 the Porsche design office was
consultant on the *Vergeltungswaffe-eins* (Revenge
Weapon One), better known to Londoners as the
V-1 buzz-bomb, a shocking footnote to Enzo
Ferrari's remark that 'Porsche don't make racing
cars, they make missiles.'

Hall *putsch*. Certainly, his autobiography was a best-seller when it appeared in Germany in 1924, perhaps because the principles of organization which pass for 'philosophy' were palatable and attractive to a nation which a few years later was willing to subjugate itself to disciplines far more strict and less moral.

Ferdinand Porsche was the embodiment of the German tradition of *Forschung*. He visited Detroit to study Henry Ford's methods and his *Volksauto* was intended as a people's car to replace people's motorbikes. It became an expression of German technical pride, but curiously the *Volks*wagen (which found acceptance everywhere) was an expression of the same culture which also gave rise to the *Volks*wohnung of National Socialist housing policies. Still, a certain Wagnerian mysticism runs through each manifestation of the Nazi ethic and is certainly still sedimented today in every Porsche: market research shows that Porsche owners have specially high loyalty to the brand on account of . . . performance, status and prestige.

In an interview with *Car* magazine on his seventy-fifth birthday, Ferry Porsche, son of the founder, explained the evolutionary design philosophy:

You must not change every year. If you do, you have the nicest car at the beginning because the changes are only made for the sake of change . . . if you change only the necessary things . . . you keep up with the competitors and keep the concept good.

It is appropriate that the first fast car to embed itself in the post-war imagination was . . . a Porsche.

When Donald Turnipseed collided one clear day in September 1955 with James Dean at the junction of Highways 41 and 46 in the Californian desert near Paso Robles and Cholame, one driver died, a myth was born and a car immortalized. The myth's components included the glamour of speed mixed with a romantic fatalism.

Turnipseed was uninjured, but James Dean was killed . . . exactly as he had expected to be. At twenty-four, Dean had just finished playing cowboy Jett Rink in *Giant* with Elizabeth Taylor and Rock Hudson, and was already a cult figure after his New York stage performance of Gide's *Immoralist* and as Cal Trask in Elia Kazan's 1954 *East of Eden*. But cars were taking over as vehicles to project his ego. The director had insisted that Dean abandon racing during production. When he and Turnipseed collided on the desert black-top, the film star was on his way at 85 mph to a race meeting at Salinas. It was history's most famous car crash.

Listen to veteran American automobile journalist, Brock Yates, describe it:

Welcome the silence. Break for a moment your bonds with time. You'll hear it first – the frantic growl of a four cam Porsche. Unmuffled. Running hard. Look into the brown-weeded hills, where the old road winds around the edge of the ravine. A tiny silver Spyder squirts into sight, lashing through the apexes, its impudent snout nipping at the wooden guardrails. Stand back as it rushes past, scrabbling for traction on the scarred macadam. Follow its raucous exhaust . . . It powers, clean and straight, speed building, toward the valley.

Far off, on the western slope, a stand of oaks marks the cafe at Cholame . . . A lone car is approaching, a black Ford two-door. It is slowing, readying for the turn. The Spyder hammers onwards, a shiny aluminium pellet aglow in the late-afternoon sun. Surely the Ford will stop. Surely the driver will spot the speeding Porsche. Surely the world of heroes and dreamy idols will not be shattered on the road to Cholame . . .

James Dean and the car, the two greater than the sum of their parts, have projected on to Yates a hidden, but nonetheless intense, impression of eroticism, the more powerful because it is not overtly expressed. The quasi-sexual vocabulary – words like clean, straight, true – is simultaneously at odds with Dean's cinema role of sullen, hulking, vulnerable brute, but suggestive of the eroticism the cinema had at that time to suppress. A time when the Californian sports car movement was at its height, when the Sports Car Club of America and the California Sports Car Club used to stage events where cars were the vehicles of desire.

The Coca-Cola ads of the mid-fifties show a world which must be very like the strutting cars and people at SCCA meets: marvellous hyper-realistic renderings document the ethology and the mating rituals of American youth. The two-place car suggested a pleasing intimacy, its high finish suggested sensuousness, its speed that recklessness associated with pre-marital sexual intercourse. The whole ensemble an elaborate parable of the relationship between fast cars, speed and physical desire.

But there was a darker side, too, as if to restore the sauce of guilt to the equation of desire = gratification. For Dean's major movie, *Rebel Without a Cause*, George Barris, a custom car designer, had worked on the hot rods. Just three days before the crash, Dean had brought his Porsche Typ 550 Spyder to Barris's Compton body shop to have racing stripes added to its lightweight German racing silver bodywork and the legend 'Little Bastard' painted on its tail . . . The proprietor recalled:

There was something strange about that particular car . . . a feeling, bad vibrations, an aura; call it what you will . . . it made me uneasy. Dean was all worked up about how he was going to race it that weekend, but I couldn't get enthusiastic about the car . . . I had crazy feelings about wanting to stop him from driving.

A succession of sinister coincidences connected with the wreckage of Dean's Porsche turned the body-shop proprietor into a believer in psychic forces. Barris bought the

The 1956 Porsche 550 Spyder. James Dean painted
the legend 'Little Bastard' on the tail of his example
and soon after was killed driving it through the
California desert. There is a curious erotic link
between violent death and sex: partly as a result of
the crash, Porsche became the most notorious and
desirable of sports cars.

wreck for $2500 with the idea of breaking the car and selling the valuable parts: a mechanic had both legs broken when the wreckage fell off the truck; a Beverly Hills doctor who acquired the engine was killed using it; another racing doctor using Dean's drive train was seriously injured when his car turned over; then, paradoxically, the wreckage was toured by the Greater Los Angeles Safety Council with admonitory notices declaring 'This Accident Could Have Been Avoided' and it was at such a show in Sacramento that the car fell off its steel plinth and broke the hip of a teenage spectator. By 1959 it was in New Orleans when it broke into its component parts while on static display. In 1968, Rolf Weutereich, Dean's mechanic and the surviving (although psychologically scarred) passenger from the fatal crash, was, according to one source, convicted of murdering his wife, according to another, he died in a road crash in Germany in 1981.

According to Brock Yates:

James Dean opened big and died bigger . . . None of them, not even Kennedy or Lennon or Presley, was mourned with more sound and fury and endless, hysterical weeping than James Dean.

Elia Kazan said he was:

highly neurotic . . . (and) . . . obviously sick.

Phil Hill said of him:

I felt he had enormous personal needs to be famous.

Ezra Goodman, a *Life* reporter, wrote of Dean:

If he thought he was not getting enough attention in a restaurant, he would beat a tom-tom solo on the tabletop, play his spoon against a water glass with a boogie beat, pour a bowl of sugar into his pocket, or set fire to a paper napkin. He collected a small crew of sycophants and what gaucheries he couldn't think of, they could.

Near his 'shrine' there is one of his favourite quotations from Saint-Exupéry's *The Little Prince*: 'What is essential is invisible to the eye'.

There is, by suggestion, a degree of exhibitionism in an actor and, besides James Dean, Steve McQueen and Paul Newman developed real accomplishment as racing drivers. In later life, their romance with machines replaced their romance with starlets. That other tragic, romantic figure of fifties America, the abstract expressionist Jackson Pollock, was killed in a car crash a little less than a year after James Dean.

Pollock, who with his technique of dripping paint across canvases was about as theatrical as a painter can get, admired Dean, at least, he once remarked 'he's fine', even though he said *Rebel Without a Cause* was 'phonied up, the psychiatric orientation oversimplified'. Drunk, depressed and driving his 1950 model Oldsmobile convertible too fast with his mistress and her girlfriend, he consummated his forty-four years of self-destruction when his car hit some Long Island trees at 10.15 one August night in 1956. The front page of the East Hampton *Star* which reported the incident on 16 August carried a photograph captioned 'Still Life'. It showed two cans of Rheingold beer, a hubcab and one of Pollock's loafers. The caption went on to say that it published the photograph 'in the hope that it may further the safer driving campaign being carried on by nation and state'. The accident transformed Pollock from a foul-mouthed, whoring, certified schizophrenic into a darling of avant-garde American chic, whose reputation was lionized in magazines such as *Life, Time* and *Newsweek* . . . whose publishers preferred their Bohemians dead. Thanks to the Oldsmobile, the Rheingold and perhaps even the girls, Pollock joined that list of sorry disappointed

After the end of the Second World War Ferdinand
Porsche was jailed by the French because of his
association with the mechanical engineering
aspects of the German war effort. Although his
health was broken during internment, with his
son, Ferry, he decided to create a sports car with
his own name. The Porsche 356 appeared in 1949.
The name derives from the design studio job
number (the Leopard tank was Porsche Typ 100).

creative people who found what they wanted in death, not in life.

According to critic Peter Fuller, given Pollock's depressive, even desperate, state of mind his death was not accidental . . . in the most neutral sense. The artist's depression was caused partly by personal factors, the shaky architecture of his character and his difficulty with relationships, but also by tensions brought about by the American Art Establishment. At exactly the time when the Museum of Modern Art propaganda machine was talking about the 'triumph of American art', with the French Impressionists merely signposts on the way from the old masters to Pollock, the artist himself was having to confront abject failure. As Fuller says, 'the only subject available to him was precisely his *inability* to find a world view'. Even as a teenager he had written:

People have always frightened and bored me, consequently I have been within my own shell and have not accomplished anything.

and

Youth – to me is a bit of damnable hell.

The favoured expressive medium of most bits of damnable hell is pop music. Although Anglo-Saxon youth culture is characterized by recurrent patterns of revolt and renewal, fuelled by a consistent and intense subversion, cars are seen as instruments of freedom as much as symbols of the hated ruling industrial class. The car song has become an established sub-category of Pop, and even a Cadillac, favoured vehicle of American plutocrats, provides a liberation motif in, for example, Bruce Springsteen's 'Cadillac Ranch':

Eldorado fins, whitewalls and skirts,
Rides just like a little bit of heaven here on earth,

59

Well buddy when I die throw my body in the back
And drive me to the junkyard in my Cadillac.

Or the Screaming Blue Messiahs' 'Twin Cadillac
Valentine', 1985:

Strong loving's what we've got
when it's hot it's hot . . .
you could be driving twin
Cadillacs at the same time
one's going 45 and one's going 99

I just live here
it's a twin Cadillac valentine
but that's no crime

Or The Clash's song:

My Baby drove up in a brand-new Cadillac
She said 'Hey, come here Daddy,
I ain't never comin back!'
'Baby, baby, won't you hear my plea?
Come on sugar, come on back to me!'
She said 'Balls to you, big daddy,
I ain't *never* comin back!'

Sex provides the explanation of the paradox. Although
not all adolescent fornication took place in pick-ups, there
is serendipity in the name. A pick-up, or better still, a
saloon car was necessary to get a girl, the cabin providing
a convenient venue for performing acts which customarily
demand an element of privacy.

In her book, *Kinflicks*, American writer Lisa Alther
makes full use of the car interior as love nest. The heroine
relates her experience with a putative and fumbling lover:

Inspired by the excess space the Mercedes back seat
offered . . . I was lying spread-eagle on the leather seat.
Joe Bob was kneeling between my legs; his miraculous
erection, finally freed, pointed at my nose as he rifled his
chino pockets with desperation.

As Lisa Alther makes clear, it's boys who drive cars. Girls, at least until very recently, do not. This is because the mating rituals of American youth demand the passivity of females. This possessiveness and the power it confers was expressed in Lennon and McCartney's 'Drive My Car', where the opportunity to control the singer's vehicle is construed as a prologue or invitation to sex.

And, according to Glenn Frey, the power has an erotic element:

I got me a car and I
    got me some gas
Told everybody they could
    kiss my ass

As Picabia had discovered sixty years before, the components of a car can be powerful sexual symbols. A world of erotic suggestion is contained in The Medallions' verse:

Would you like to go riding
In my Buick '59?
I said, would you like to go riding
In my Buick '59?
It's got two carburettors
And a supercharger up the side.

or The Beach Boys':

With Naugahyde bucket seats in front and back,
Everything is chrome, man, even my jack.

The erotic, if unconscious, implications are clear. The only exceptions to this rule, at least as expressed in Pop, fall outside the mainstream of rock: Grace Jones' version of 'Warm Leatherette' highlights the sado-erotic elements of a car crash. The use of 'Leatherette' itself provides an interesting period detail. Since the very early seventies cars have had velour seats and the evocation of this ancient substance suggests conscious nostalgia. It is a truism that people feel a nostalgia most intense for the decade in which they were born. Expressions of nostalgia by contemporary exponents of pop culture look back to America in the fifties.

Beyond personal associations, this Golden Age seems to have an almost universal appeal. The image of the car as it is fixed in popular culture is a Chevy, a Ford or a Cadillac. Not a Peugeot, even in France. Yet, interestingly, American car styling has not been able to sustain its allure beyond this Golden Age of the fifties, the decade when America was truly prosperous. By the sixties it had lost direction and by the eighties it had become a cruel parody of itself. The car is, of course, a curiously precise tool for calibrating cultural values. With the United States losing prestige in the international arena, American car styling went to hell.

5 STYLING
La Bella Figura

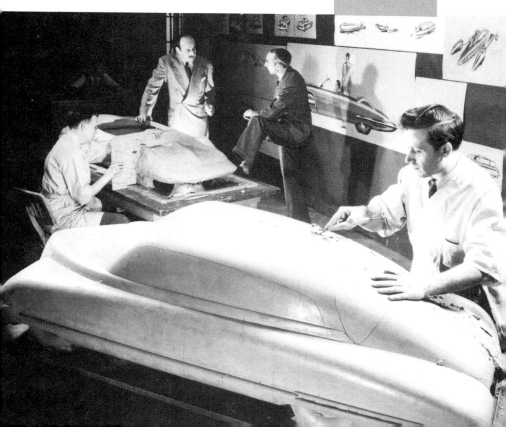

One sunny day in the twenties General Motors realized that people bought cars not just as transport but for looks. The result was billions of man-hours getting invested in styling, or creative effort intended to influence and second guess popular taste. Thousands of artisans made clay models for management to scrutinize. Shortly afterwards, these sculptors' fantasies were in the showrooms.

In terms of styling and popular appeal, American cars betrayed their own fine tradition. While the mass-market manufacturers had got rich by stimulating and satisfying demand, they lost their way. It was clever stuff while it lasted, but replete with success and complacent about the Japanese threat, they fell behind the game, fat and exhausted in the mid-seventies. In about 1975, for the first time ever, a spectre arose saying no one owed Detroit a living. At first no one understood. No one in Detroit, that is, but the American public was on the ball. It even seemed that the really famous names might go and join Packard and Studebaker the other side of the Styx.

Ford's Lincoln division was one of the chief contributors to this massive public revulsion against the American car. Lincoln used to like to supply the sort of thing which looked fine at a spangled, Dralon resort hotel in the Catskills where they measure a car's worth by the length of its hood, but it would mean society death if you were to drive off the Nantucket and Martha's Vineyard ferry in one. Here, and on Long Island, where smart Manhattan residents weekend, a 1974 Honda Civic had more prestige than a Lincoln Town Car, tricked out like a face-lifted Rodeo Drive matron in the faddish inventions of 'designer' names, Bill Blass, Emilio Pucci and Valentino.

American geography was directly responsible for the fatal provincialism of its motor industry: Detroit, which is north of some parts of Canada, is a huge distance from California. Motown executives would fly out to the coast and observe that people actually liked buying Volkswagens, Volvos and Japanese cars, but by the time they

In 1979 Ford's Lincoln division commissioned
'designer' versions of the luxury 'Town Car', to
appeal to the Rodeo Drive set who had just started
getting used to having signatures on their jeans.
With Bill Blass (and Emilio Pucci and Valentino)
they could have signatures on their cars as well.
Three years later, Ford of Europe introduced the
Sierra (inset), an altogether more subtle and
sophisticated exercise in automobile design.
Instead of selling glitz, Ford now sold high
technology.

got back on the plane to the mid-West and left the Californian sunshine behind them, the car of the future was just a memory. It must be just like the image of bougainvillaea for the Mediterranean holidaymakers de-planing at Luton. When they got back to Detroit they just got back to concentrating on the length of the hood and increasing the razzle-dazzle.

And they got ignored. Suddenly, American cars found themselves with a hugh credibility problem in their own back yard. A study by the Institute of Social Research at the University of Michigan showed that between 1968 and 1975 'quality' became twice as important a factor to Americans buying new cars. One of the first responses to the public's demand for better design was the Lincoln Mk VII LSC, a car which contained a lot of the old problems, but also a nourishing amount of the solution.

The big car can be whoossshhhed and hustled through London traffic with surprising ease and, while not fast against the clock, if you floor it and engage the kickdown it's like selecting Full Surge at a medium-sized hydro-electric plant. You get swept along on a wave of awesome momentum. Aesthetically, the proportions are distin-guished (I think the designers were shown a blurred Polaroid of a Mercedes-Benz and told to get on with it) and the car has a massive elegance which is spoilt only by the odd, unbearable flourish of Detroit Baroque. Even though they *know* the American car buyers want tight, hard German cars, somewhere in Ford's management there are still people who believe they were doing it right all along. Only this sort of thinking can explain a ridiculous pseudo-hump to accommodate a spare wheel which is, in fact, stowed horizontally at the forward end of the car. Unless, that is, they employ Post-Modern architects in Dearborn.

But, absurd as much of it is to European eyes, the

appearance of the big Lincoln had an important symbolic significance: it was the first American car since the famed, but unsuccessful, Chrysler Airflow, to acknowledge the importance of *aerodynamics*.

Ferdinand Piech made Audi into the most technologically advanced car manufacturer in Europe by concentrating first of all on that very subject, but his British advertising agency, Bartle Bogle Hegarty, was concerned that the pressures of aerodynamic research were tending to make all cars look the same and, therefore, unmarketable. According to Jeremy Judge of BBH, they were sitting in a meeting room in Audi's Bavarian headquarters at Ingolstadt. Piech, speaking slowly and fixing the agency's men with a gimlet eye, said, 'Are ze birdies all the same? And ze fishes?'

Birds, fishes and vehicles all have to move through fluids, either water or air. Moving vehicles upset air, putting it into unnecessary motion. As air is surprisingly heavy, this wastes energy: the turbulence causes a friction known as drag and it is the aim of aerodynamic research to reduce it. That's one way the Lincoln got to look so clever and technological, giving its customers that feeling of *quality* they craved. Aerodynamics is a science (if an imperfect one) and streamlining is the manifestation of it in form. Looking back through history, you can see that the pursuit of aerodynamic efficiency has, interestingly, produced very many beautiful shapes; clearly, it is a science which inspires designers.

The first streamlined cars were racers, in fact designed for Austro-Daimler by Ferdinand Porsche in 1910. At that stage, Porsche still hadn't done all his *Forschung* and it took Paul Jaray to make it scientific. Jaray's obsession was 'penetration' and it was under his influence that Bugatti built his 'Tank' racers in 1924, with their upper bodies removed so as to reduce drag. Jaray's work was continued by Wunibald Kamm, whose extensive wind tunnel research produced a rich vocabulary of form, particularly the K-Body with the cut-off tail. At the same time, his theory that good 'penetration' depended on the lowest interrupted cross-section led to the widespread introduction of dramatically sloped windscreens which are still with us today.

It is not surprising that a nation as keen on *Forschung* as the Germans developed car designs arising out of scientific data gathered in the wind tunnel. The Italians were altogether more intuitive, doing theirs in the sculptor's studio. The great Italian *carrozzerie* arose out of coachbuilding traditions going back to Roman chariots. Of the big names – Bertone, Boneschi, Coggiola, Coriasco, Fissore, Frua, Ghia, ItalDesign, Moretti, Zagato – the biggest, proudest aand best is Pininfarina, founded in 1912. As if to amplify the sculptural traditions of the everyday Lombard or Piedmont *carrozzeria*, at the back of its *Lessico della Carrozzeria* Pininfarina publishes tables of illustrations: looking at the careful line drawings of the *lardon, tas á cheur, scopel mocc, batoir, rimboror* and *decopar*, you do not know whether you are in a car factory or looking at the inventory of a sculptor's atelier. In fact, the Pininfarina people talk about their massive industrial facility at Grugliasco as a 'sculpture' factory, a fact which tells you as much about Italian culture as the scrotal leather and bankscript graphics on the Lincoln's driver's manual tells you about the American.

In his autobiography, *Nato con l'automobile* (1968), Battista Farina explains how he liked to buff up his mother's casseroles. The fundamental form of the *marmite* inspired Picasso and gave to the young Farina a keen sense of sculptural form. As a car designer he was at first influenced by the massive sweeping lines of American cars, whose influence can be seen in his Lancia Astura

67

Bocca of 1937, but the almost innate sculptural sensibility took over. Ignorant of Kamm's theories, but expert on *la passegiata* and the eternal concept of *la bella figura*, Farina started inclining windscreens just before the Second World War.

From 1945 he worked with Piero Dusio and their Cisitalia is now, appropriately for sculpture, the sole car in New York's Museum of Modern Art. It led to the creation of what some people consider to be the most beautiful car of all time, the 1951 Lancia B20 Gran Turismo, the original popular 'fastback' whose lines, simultaneously nervous and sober, influenced generations of imitators, including plenty by Farina himself. If one car is more beautiful than the Lancia B20 it is the Ferrari Dino 206 of 1969, where nervousness and sobriety are replaced by animal curves and the tension of sinew.

Pininfarina's successor is Giorgetto Giugiaro, a relative newcomer to the *carrozzeria* business. His success in the workmanlike design of the Volkswagen Golf and the Fiat Panda made his ItalDesign company rich and gave him the freedom and opportunity to start designing crash helmets, cameras, clothes and even spaghetti. Uwe Bahnsen, chief designer of Ford, says:

I think he is stretching himself. Pasta and trousers and cameras. Because of his reputation, I believe the demand on his services is very high, so he comes up every two or three years with an interesting concept and makes minor variations and sells it all over the world. The Lotus Esprit is dramatic only because of its proportions, not because of its design.

I asked Uwe Bahnsen why the Italians are so bad at making big cars. He replied:

Some sarcastic individual once remarked that Fiat production cars are designed so that even the most mediocre coachbuilder can improve on them! It's partly

68

Pininfarina's bodywork for the Ferrari Dino 206 of
1969 is a masterpiece of the coachbuilder's art.
Lean and spare, yet overtly sensual, it defined the
shape of the modern sports car.

the way the Italian motor industry works. They don't have large in-house design activities: they buy it in.

Designers are often pretty sharp about their rivals' creations. Although Bahnsen's admiration for Giugiaro is moderate, Giugiaro can himself be scathing. It is reported that when he first saw Harris Mann's dreadful Triumph TR7 with its ugly scalloped sides he took one look and said 'My God! Don't tell me they've done that to the other side as well.'

Appreciation of the styling of cars is the nearest most of us ever get to the consumption of art. Since General Motors' discovery of styling in the twenties, no manufacturer in a free market who has wanted to stay in business has been able to avoid it. Although the days of Detroit's underbraked, cart-sprung barges are over and while there is no Harley Earl to lay on chrome with a trowel, the system is much the same. Only the names of the personalities have changed and they have swopped media. The itch of demand can still be excited by the automobile stylist, although nowadays his repertoire of techniques is more subtle.

When Flaminio Bertoni's Citroën DS was first displayed at the Paris Motor Show of 1955, it was mounted without its wheels, on a pylon, lest the vulgar necessity of road wheels compromise the public's perception of it as fiercely beautiful sculpture. It was the sight of this big new Citroën that inspired Roland Barthes' famous essay. The car, known as 'DS' (a contraction of the factory code name 'Voiture de Grande Diffusion'), came to be known as the *Déesse*, or Goddess, confirming Barthes' assumptions about the role of imagery in modern life.

Cars are the most familiar of industrial society's products, yet at the same time the most evocative, the most desirable. In them you can see invested all the skills and anxieties of our age. Just as medieval cathedrals used symbolic sculpture and mysterious harmonic proportions to encode the beliefs of their civilization, so car designers do in ours. In the Middle Ages everybody worshipped in a cathedral. Nowadays, everybody worships in the car park.

If this sounds far-fetched, consider the orthodox company. Here a rigid formalism operates, as hieratic as anything contrived by the medieval church. In a British public company the chairman will have a Jaguar. This is usually parked by the main doors, right in front of Reception. The chairman does not have to suffer the humiliation of having to find his parking space filled by the Xerox service van. Besides the chairman's Jaguar, in bays marked 'Reserved' you will find the senior directors' Rovers and the more junior directors' Ford Granadas. There are no variations on this scheme.

A design consultant, who might well be visiting this same company, will explain that he cannot afford *not* to have a BMW because his clients expect it. After he has done his presentation in Crawley, his clients will walk with him to the car park. Quite literally, they want to see the cut of his metal. If he shimmied into, say, a Talbot Horizon, he would not give a convincing impression of being a man in charge of his own destiny, still less of being a man of taste and discernment. *L'homme bien pensant et de bon volonté*, if he is in business on his own account, drives a German car. Drive something less and you declare to your world in a sculptured ton of metal calling card that I do not care about style, appearance, chic, sex. This would be fine for a Benedictine novice or a virgin from Surbiton, but it is poor, thin stuff for an ambitious designer.

There *are* some alternatives to German cars: a Citroën Mehari plastic jeep would create an impression of Bohemian insouciance which might just have swung the job and a Rolls-Royce is still, despite the decline in quality and the descent into Highgate-Bedouin taste, an im-

The Citroën DS became known as the 'Goddess' because the phonic slip from a contraction of 'voiture de grande diffusion' gave rise, spoken in French, to *Déesse*. At its first appearance in Paris, 1955, the highly advanced Citroën astonished the press and the public. Once shown without wheels (so that rude mechanicals did not compromise perception of its astonishing shape), the Citroën gave rise to Roland Barthes' most famous essay in which he wrote 'cars . . . are our cathedrals.' The car was presented to the French public on the pages of *Paris Match* by Gina Lollobrigida.

pressive, if contemptuous, token that you have money to burn. But after a decade and a half of relentless marketing, a BMW gives off very safe aromas. Its drivers inhabit a world of ski holidays and expensive dry cleaners. The perfect pleats and folds and tucks, the lapidary finish, are tangible evidence of order and of the discriminating disbursement of ample funds.

BMW has always been promoted by aggressive and clever advertising campaigns. In the sixties and seventies the company established for itself a reputation for dynamic aggression with a series of ads which showed a rear-view mirror full of charging BMW, lights on main beam with the loutishly assertive copyline 'Move Over For BMW'. This campaign established for the Bavarian bubble car and motor-bike manufacturer a reputation for aggressiveness with which the estate agents and account-ants (who formed a large proportion of the customer profile) were happy to identify.

The pushy and irresponsible 'Move Over . . .' cam-paign was replaced by the calmer, yet perhaps more insidious, advertisements of Wight Collins Rutherford Scott. WCRS carefully nurtured the image of the BMW owner not so much as a blood-crazed tearaway but as the archetype of Thatcherite professional man. Look at the ads and you'll see: he works in Milton Keynes, goes skiing, understands electronics and lives in an architect-designed house. He is less aggressive because it is an age which is more civilized, more mature. The image is impressive and, no doubt, persuasive, but increasingly hard to maintain in the face of the fact that burgeoning production of BMWs means that the precious currency, so shrewdly contrived, is being debased every time a Rasta drives an old 3.oSi through Neasden with his in-car boom-box doing Captain Kite and the High Flyers.

The tiny slot in the market-place which BMW and its

ad men so cleverly prised open has left them vulnerable in image terms now that they have vacated niches lower down the scale for competitors to inhabit. One such niche was inhabited by customizers.

Customizing is the enhancement of production machinery by aftermarket additions. Once it was known only to America's West Coast and London east of the Dartford Tunnel, but soon it became culturally acceptable because consumers longed to break out of the constraints put upon them by the economies of scale of mass-production which creates millions of identical products. As soon as they learnt the lesson, manufacturers themselves started to ape the customizers' lesson and produce speciality cars. One of the first manifestations was . . . white cars.

Here, in what the marketing people call the discretionary part of the market-place, cars are bought as gifts. Convertibles are specially popular because they have that toy-like quality you expect in a gift: something genuinely unnecessary, yet nevertheless intensely pleasurable. Volkswagen has traditionally sold convertibles at Christmas. Children enjoy playing with things which have flaps, lids and doors and it may well be that the folding lid of the all-white convertible provokes an unconscious reminiscence of childhood pleasure. It's rather reminiscent of Peter Behrens' old dictate that 'a motor *should* be like a birthday present' . . .

The subjective use of colour should be seen in this context. Once colours were used on racing cars: green for Britain, red for Italy, blue for France, but the present vogue for white cars taps a deeper meaning. White has such a potent symbolic force that the effect of an all-white car is very different to the effect of an all-black one: in the all-white, the fashion-conscious wear trademark sunglasses, in all-black the fascist-conscious can pretend they're in the Wehrmacht. Just as a white room accentuates

It is a paradox that in an age of restricted
economic growth manufacturers produce
ostentatiously conspicuous all-white cars. Market
research shows they are often bought as gifts while
personal observation suggests they are bought by
exhibitionists. Their popularity amongst
consumers with large 'discretionary' incomes
emphasizes the continued symbolic role of the
motor car in modern industrial civilization.

its contents, giving every little bitty detail a centre-stage prominence, so a white car accentuates its driver. Black cars are like sculpture, made to be admired from afar by their owners and others. A white car is like an empty canvas and you, the owner, are going to be the daub. If you're lucky, you'll be a *Bella Figura*.

6 DESIGN
The Mobile Environment

The car interior is a perfect little environment where nothing has happened by accident but a lot has by design. People who live at home with half-timbered freezers, pokerwork decoration and televisions like provincial French armoires can live in a car where everything is intelligent, technical and artificial. This Lancia was designed by Milanese architect Mario Bellini.

Static controlled environment is called architecture. Mobile controlled environment is called a car. The interior of an automobile is like architecture without architects. A journalist recently calculated that many Americans spend an amount of time in their cars that is only exceeded by the amount of time they spend in bed. It is not surprising that a decisive factor in an individual's decision to buy a particular car is often the interior design, as much as the thrill of promised speed, or the social satisfaction given by a brand, or the sexual arousal stimulated by an artfully contrived orifice, pleat or curve. While shapes communicate ideas, interiors create atmosphere. Many people, unconscious experts in interior design, buy cars as *environment.*

Inside a car you get a perfect little exercise in interior design, a controlled environment better than most homes. People who would never go to the expense of buying trademark imported furniture, carpets and curtains, who wouldn't even know how to begin to call in a lighting consultant or hire an interior designer, make discriminating choices in car showrooms.

There are people who, at home, have Great Exhibition floral carpets, purple Dralon suites, prints of Big Ben or wild animals, a music centre, DHSS lighting, the *AA Book of the Road*, stale air, ornaments, processed food, German wine, white bread, artificial fabrics, and novels by Jeffrey Archer, who enjoy, when they are on the road, the sober, controlled environment of their Nissan Cherry where colours and details have been meticulously thought out, cost-controlled down to the last decimal of a yen. They sit in an injection-moulded technical womb on a seat designed ergonomically, the air purified for them, fed information by dials and read-outs made in Nagoya or Yokohama. This Nissan Cherry has better interior design than any home you can think of costing less than about a quarter of a million. It is a little world so neat that nothing could be added to or subtracted from it without impairing the effect contrived by the man from Nagoya.

After being in a building, the experience of being in cars is our most familiar contact with design. Historically speaking, technological development and the inevitable push of market forces has accelerated the progress in car design. Walter Dorwin Teague, one of the first men to open a design consultancy (in New York in the 1920s), noted as early as 1940 that:

The automobile manufacturers have made, in the past few years, a greater contribution to the art of comfortable seating than chair builders in all preceding history.

The rate of change of progress is now beginning to accelerate. Car interiors are really on the move. Just as the first radios, when they became available in the twenties, were made to look like furniture (because that was the only vaguely familiar reference point their designers could think of), the earliest car interiors were made to feel like being in regular architecture. It was Jules Verne who first fantasized that cars would be like mobile houses and since then architecture and cars have been in a curiously fertile relationship.

It was automobile assembly lines that inspired the paean to 'Fordism' in Le Corbusier's *Vers une Architecture* and it must surely have been the sight of so many perfect little environments rolling off the end of the River Rouge track that inspired his hackneyed, but still heroic, trope that houses should be *machines for living in.* Cars had already achieved that condition.

Perhaps more than any other artefact, cars require more sustained design input at every level. As a consequence, they can be 'read' more thoroughly than anything, except, perhaps, a building. In 1928, Le Corbusier, taking a moment off the prosecution of the Modern Movement, even designed a compact car. His drawing shows an adventurous little vehicle, which calls to mind comparisons with Pierre Boulanger's Citroën Deux Chevaux (which did not, in fact, appear until a decade later). Interestingly, when Le Corbusier's great German rival, Walter Gropius, designed some car architecture for Adler in 1931, three years after he resigned the directorship of the Bauhaus, the result was a handsome and dignified car, but an anachronistic design. Strangely for someone as obsessed with functionalism and mass production as Gropius, his Adler was hand-made; its massive lines reveal an imagination closer in spirit to a Neo-Classical temple than to the image of factory buildings evoked by Le Corbusier's contemporary design.

Although the 'traditional' British car interior, with its walnut and leather, is modelled on assumptions about country house architecture best understood by Jungian analysts (but confirming C.P. Snow's observation that nine out of ten British 'traditions' date from the second half of the nineteenth century), other influences have joined architecture in the evolution of the car interior. These influences have rarely been avant-garde, perhaps because automobile production has often occurred in military towns which had manufacturing experience of making armaments: it is no coincidence that Turin, home of the Italian motor industry, also houses Piedmont's greatest arsenal. Similarly, André Citroën made munitions on Paris's Quai de Javel before he made cars there.

But while military experience influenced the technological development of cars, it could have little effect on the evolution of their interiors. In fact, it is remarkable how

79

much at odds with military practice the familiar car interior has turned out to be. The Institute of Aviation Medicine in the Royal Aircraft Establishment at Farnborough has published papers which describe experiments in the early post-war years where a Gloster Meteor was fitted out with a pilot's environment which required him to adopt a prone position so as to give him better comfort and increased control. No such experiment has ever been made with a car. Similarly, the Royal Air Force always uses rearward facing passenger seats in its transport aircraft because it is safer and more comfortable, the body and the seat working in harmony to ensure that any g forces that occur work benignly. Passengers in commercial airliners resist rearward facing seats because of the pull of tradition. In the case of cars, the cultural inheritance from architecture has produced conservative designs: people sit up and face forward, rather as they do in armchairs in a drawing room.

Yet increasing competition, squeezed margins and over-populated markets have required manufacturers to use advanced interior design as a means of exciting a customer's cupidity and, therefore, his itch to *buy*. Environment is playing an ever more important role in motivating sales: it is suspected that most people buy Japanese cars straight off the showroom floor, without actually driving them.

Interior design, when it applies to cars, can be broadly divided into (1) ergonomics (the study of man's physical relationship to his work) and (2) style, where it is possible to separate them. In some cases, friction between the two apparently distinct areas of scientific and artistic activity is helping to bring about another sort of planned obsolescence, thirty years after the first dynamic round. This version of it is not solely concerned with symbolic motifs but more with the apparent value of the ergonomics. Giorgetto Giugiaro, founder of ItalDesign and the man who created the architecture of the Volkswagen Golf, the Alfa-Sud and the Fiat Panda admits to using the same perversion of evolution that Harley preached in the fifties. In explaining why his emphasis had shifted from long, low, sleek sporty cars to upright, boxy ones he told *Business Week* 'I have to eat, you know'.

Ergonomics is a multi-disciplinary pseudo-science as imperfectly understood inside a car as aerodynamics is without. It is more a case of being fairly sure what you must not do, than of being scientifically certain about what is and what is not correct: it would require an osteopath with a degree in social anthropology adequately to explain why Germans demand seats in their cars which are like blocks of concrete, while the French prefer the velour embrace of a foam-filled dollop of sculptured industrial ectoplasm, lacking entirely any supportive structure. Despite what Walter Dorwin Teague had to say, Americans until very recently insisted on having glossy plastic 'bench' seats (perhaps to remind them of diners, another possible inheritance from architecture for the motor industry) and still manufacture cars whose 'head' rests sit somewhere just below the shoulder blades.

Vance Packard and Ralph Nader began to change this. The seventies oil shock finalized the process. It was just after 1973 that Giugiaro began to move his design emphasis away from the low-slung towards the hitherto unsung box on wheels, although ten years or so before that, American designer Charles Eames had said that the London perpendicular taxi cab was the most perfect essay in industrial design that he had ever known. Increasing petrol prices brought about space efficiency, socially responsible, ingenious-rather-than-irresponsibly-beautiful designs. His Megagamma concept car created waves of imitators and derivatives: the Volvo LCP, the Nissan

Prairie, Honda City, Fiat Uno and the new American driveable vans. In some respects, the advanced popular car of today is more like a London cab than a Lockheed combat plane.

But despite the clear ergonomic advantages of building tall, boxy cars, it is still *style* rather than function which dominates vehicle interior design. To continue the parallel with building: 'Architecture', Friedrich von Schelling once remarked, 'is in general like frozen music'. Continuing the assumption that car interiors are an effective parody of architecture, you can divide their style rather as you can divide the history of music. That is to say, into useful abstract categories: 'early', 'classical', 'modern' and 'avant-garde'.

'Early' interiors subdivide into two categories: one is primitive, as in Eastern European cars where Russian low technology is combined with an artlessly misunderstood ragbag of dated, wretched American and Italian styling clichés. The second category is the simple, yet sophisticated, interior of the Citroën Deux Chevaux, a model of how intelligent design and restrained execution can result in an effect that is both functional and *chic*. Genuinely fresh ideas like those of the Citroën do not date: Giugiaro's Fiat Panda, ingenious in its own way, is a reinterpretation of the Bauhaus rationale that inspired the Citroën's simple geometric shapes and *Existenzminimum* industrial details.

'Classical' car interiors might be considered those which have derived their inspiration from technical sources, in order to give the owner an exciting feeling of being close to professionalism and perfection: inside a Porsche the dials are so huge and clear you can fancy yourself in the control room of a North Sea U-boat pen. In Sweden, Saab's Bjorn Envall has said that he took a long look at the Viggen interceptor aircraft before he designed the dashboard of the 900. BMW, too, has been inspired by aerospace practice: the nocturnal red glow in a Bavarian *Mittelklasse* 'dynamic environment' is intended to evoke an aura of expertise, so shrewdly exploited in other fields by the company's marketing staff and its advertising agency. It was BMW that Ford had in mind when the impressive interior of the Sierra was designed: as if to emphasize the symbolic importance of 'expertise' in this area of car styling, the design staff was briefed 'to make the driver *feel* important'.

The 'modern' idiom in car interiors is not yet fully resolved in its search for and acquisition of symbols. Lancia employs architect Mario Bellini, Italy's leading product designer. He has produced genuinely weird instrument panels for the second generation Beta, a complex moulding reminiscent of an internal component of a past machine. But of European companies it is, perhaps, Renault who most effectively imitates the Japanese 'Tokyo-by-night' school: chief designer, Robert Opron, pays serious attention to the interior even if he sometimes does not achieve serious results. Ford's Uwe Bahnsen says that the interior of the R25 looks as though it has had two stages of the development process left out of it: its weird re-entrant angles, like the *guichets* on the *péage* section of French autoroutes, came straight from the model-maker's fibre-board. Renault details are less subtle than dramatic: the flagship of the range has more switches, knobs, slides, levers, buttons and diodes than anything short of the aft cabin of the Rockwell B1-B. Many of these are used to control the awesome in-car entertainment system which alone requires a sixteen-page explanatory booklet!

It is in the area of the 'avant-garde' that the most extraordinary experiments take place, although few of them have had any value beyond amusement. Some years ago the great Milanese designer, Ettore Sottsass, was commissioned by his friend, Elio Fiorucci, to re-work an

Alfa-Romeo Giulietta. Sottsass, an architect whose career began with low-cost housing for the INA-Casa schemes during Italy's post-war *ricostruzione*, matured into an irreverent, ironical and quixotic figure who specialized in subverting popular assumptions about the nature of familiar things. 'Why should homes be static temples?' he asked. In pursuit of the same subversion he decided that cars were too aggressive and inhuman, so he painted the sporty Alfa with huge spots and inside he laid Astroturf on the floor and painted clouds on the headlining so that the occupants might feel more *natural*. Alfa-Romeo had it scrapped.

The intentional irony, even subversion, of this design exercise was specially Italian. Uwe Bahnsen explains about national characteristics and how they effect car design:

There have been distinct national identities in car design, but I believe that for the moment, at least for the past fifteen years, it has been less and less so. I sense a certain re-occurrence, in some markets at least, of a national identity. I believe that this is a reaction to the levelling out of design standards of world markets. The two latest Mercedes models, the 190 and the W124, are very much within the classic tradition of Mercedes. They are both a very Teutonic interpretation of a modern trend. They could not have come out of France or Britain.

What actually is it that makes Mercedes cars look so essentially German?

I think it's an interpretation of a message communicated through the shape. It's a very conscious design philosophy which aims to create a visual solidity which communicates what the company stands for. Not terribly sophisticated because I think there is a German tradition which is solid and not necessarily terribly refined which these cars to some degree represent. If you look at these two designs you will see that every radius of sheet metal is very deliberately determined. It is not designed, let's say, to the minimum achievable with the material. Mercedes' metal gauge is probably nought point seven five, or eight five, the same as everybody else's, but it is purposely designed to look two millimetres. You cannot bend two-millimetre steel tighter than a certain radius and I believe Mercedes-Benz are trying consciously to achieve that effect. A 190 or a W124 looks unbelievably solid. It is supportive of the Mercedes corporate image of absolute solidity, quality and durability. The design underlines that very consciously. There is something typically German in that interpretation. It's a lack of playful refinement. Everything is very sheer, very bold.

Mercedes-Benz has a very clever and intelligent marketing strategy. I believe in many ways that marketing is as undiscovered an activity as design once was. At the launch of the 190 something quite unexpected happened in Germany. During the first six to eight months, almost the whole of the production was base cars with the smallest engine with not one extra, not even a rear view mirror. The cars were bought by people who had aspired to own a Mercedes all their lives and now finally *a car has come down into the region they could afford!* At this point Mercedes started to get worried about their image: suddenly, while trying to pick up the aspiring younger executives with a small car, they had created a car bought by people at retirement age. Then they had this very clever idea of putting a Cosworth engine and spoilers and skirts onto the 190 and within a very short time they also encouraged some of the more serious body shop converters to supply aftermarket additions to the extent that the 190 now enjoys the image the 3 Series BMW once enjoyed and I would say that in Germany more than half of the 190s running around have some sort of converter element so that Mercedes have managed again to shift back to where they wanted to be.

The state of the art of car design in any country is not only a means of precisely calibrating the health of its culture, but mirrors exactly the obsessions of the age. When in the 1930s quality and reliability were paramount characteristics of a motor vehicle, coachbuilt cars aped the architecture of grand hotels and country houses. There is not a great deal to choose between sitting in a James Young Rolls-Royce or in the lobby of The Connaught. In the sixties, with Mini-Coopers doing well in international competitions, it was *chic* (at least in certain parts of Britain), to have a car which suggested that you too were taking part in the Monte Carlo rally. By the seventies, Volvo had defined the consumer's taste for environmental protection and in our own decade, technology itself, even in caricatured form, is what sells cars.

7 MARKETING
Vorsprung durch Technik

Photographer Jacques-Henri Lartigue had a passion for automobiles. In an age of indulged innocence for the Mediterranean set, cars were not mere consumer durables. Treated as sculpture—as in this 1927 picture taken near the Italian border—cars have a place as secure in Lartigue's iconography as guitars and bottles in Braque's and Picasso's.

There can be no better evidence that marketing is an imperfect science than the extraordinary fact that when he was booted out of Detroit for creating the Edsel, a $250m loss-maker and the industry's greatest disaster, the first thing Roy Brown did when he set up in Ford's Siberia at Dagenham was to design the Ford Cortina. Perhaps because of the Cortina, he is remembered as remarking unselfconsciously to a colleague 'I have so much talent it frightens me.'

The Cortina was the first car in Europe to emerge from the process called *product planning*. This signalled an end to the idea that cars, like any other designs, were the result of autonomous acts of creative will. Even as late as 1960, at least in the British motor industry, fundamental design and engineering decisions were made as a personal whim or fiat of the managing director or chairman, according to the convictions and taste of the person who owned the plant. Like the invention of 'design' itself, at the end of the industrial revolution, product planning was yet another stage in the division of labour. Cars were now to be massaged, packaged and marketed like soap powder, only unlike soap powder they were complicated and the planning business surrounding them was correspondingly complicated too.

As manufacturers began to see Europe as an integral market, rather than as a geography book collection of countries, product planning became one of the most significant decision-making processes in the motor industry. The Cortina was code-named the Archbishop and its product planning team was led by Terry Beckett, now

Sir Terence Beckett of the Confederation of British Industry. Under Beckett the rules were established and detailed analysis of the competition (together, if possible, with a clandestine inside line) became customary. It was after detailed analysis of the technologically advanced BMC Mini, which Ford established couldn't possibly be produced at a profit, that the parameters for the Archbishop were established. A process of competitive comparative analysis among Ford engineers, who signed off the achievement of specific objectives in a 'Red Book', lasted three and a half months and then the planners were able to give the engineers cost and weight targets for each component. At a cost of a mere £13m, this process gave rise to the Ford Cortina in 1962.

The Cortina was a meticulously conceived modern transport package, using conventional engineering design, but manufactured in a sophisticated way. As a product it seemed to fill the consumer's material and metaphysical needs, becoming Britain's most successful consumer product. Its magic formula was to offer the customer some of the superficially attractive idioms of American car styling within overall dimensions that were European standard in terms of compactness and efficiency. Although through half-closed eyes, it looked like a Detroit compact, the Cortina attracted people because it was a modern European car. The name played an important, if unconscious part in this recognition process. While a previous generation of British cars had been named after tweedy old university towns, Oxford and Cambridge, for instance, this new Ford was named after Cortina d'Ampezzo, the North Italian hill town that hosted the 1960 Winter Olympics. This gave the first generation of British tourists to benefit from cheap jet travel a tangible symbol of European awareness to park in their drives. Soon, other attractions besides the Cortina's cosmopolitanism were presented to beguile the consumer, among them the virtues of reliability, safety, longevity and quality.

These were, of course, the very virtues which advertising copywriter, David Abbott, identified for Volvo. Their advertising is a long-term campaign, building on Volvo's virtues rather than denying its vices of dullness and ugliness. Abbott, who has written more than ninety Volvo ads, says these qualities were always built into the Volvo product, and now, after ten years of successful advertising, they are also built into the Volvo driver. Abbott's own agency, Abbott Mead Vickers, also handles the account of Sainsbury's, the supermarket chain: his esoteric control over the values and images of a certain section of the British middle class is almost total: if you ask children at primary school to draw a Volvo, they draw the estate car version. The one you see in Sainsbury's car parks. As Abbott says:

The marketing trick that Volvo has pulled off is that they don't want to be all things to all men, or women. They have about three or four per cent of the UK market and that's a very nice piece of business.

Abbott thinks that the Volvo has never been a pretty car, so Volvo owners believe they are making a *rational* choice, a decision between heart and mind. In the United States they even ran a tag line on Volvo: 'The car for people who think'. It is, as David Abbott puts it, the prestige of intellect rather than the prestige of money.

If you get seventy per cent of your buyers coming back on a two or three-year cycle, a significant percentage of your sales are to people who have already bought the Volvo message and a large part of your advertising is reinforcing that belief. It is a religious job. The important principle here is that most car advertising is aimed at people who have already bought the car! According to Abbott:

AN 18 YEAR-OLD VOLVO AND TWO OF ITS CONTEMPORARIES.

VBW 736

It is not only the imagery of sex and worldly success which sells cars. Volvos are enthusiastically consumed because their advertising has consistently made a virtue of their doleful, passive virtues. It is Abbott Mead Vickers, the agency which creates the thoughtful and informative ads for the definitively middle-class Sainsbury supermarket chain, who handles Volvo.

Advertising reassures them in their choice and they become evangelists for the marque . . . The product is the hero of the advertising.

As in all religious systems, one ikon supplements another. By the 1980s, with safety established as a desirable asset, the public had become willing, even eager, to accept *technology* as an attribute in car design. While in ages past this or that inflection of a stylist's whim had given us tail fins and chrome, or a 'Gran Turismo' Ford Cortina, the results of the various oil crises combined with the vast shake-out of industry which left the globe with but a handful of major manufacturers meant that technology, or, at least, the appearance of it, was the additive necessary to excite the consumer's desire to acquire.

Two cars which appeared in 1982 summarized the changed mood. Although one was mass-market and the other was more exclusive, they were both evidence of the same phenomenon. The first was the Ford Sierra, the second was the Audi 100.

The Ford Sierra was launched twenty years to the day after the Ford Cortina. The difference was that European sales of Japanese cars in 1962 had been a thousand, but by 1982 they were a million. Just as the Cortina arose out of a self-conscious product planning process, so the Sierra arose out of another self-conscious process, in this case, Ford's 'After Japan Programme', a consciousness-raising exercise intended to equip the company to combat the Japanese. The problem was that, even given the degree of robotics and automation available in Japanese factories, cultural differences between the Japanese and the Europeans meant that Ford could not possibly compete on price alone. They chose something else: technology, or, at least, the appearance of it. They had decided that it was no longer a Cortina 1.6L world. The consumer demanded technology. He was more sophisticated than someone who bought a car named after a ski resort. One response to this was Ford's brief to the Sierra's interior designers: 'you've got to make the driver feel *important*.' In terms of its significance to the history of marketing, this instruction rivals Clairol's immortal hair-dye copyline: 'If I have one life, let me live it as a blonde.'

According to its designer, Uwe Bahnsen, the Sierra is:

a distinctly European design statement, clearly setting Ford apart from this homogenous mass of indistinguishable interpretations to which the Japanese have contributed so much. We wanted to create an identity, a focal point. The essence of the concept is to create a new platform in car design from which to break out of the mask, get yourself onto a new platform and communicate what you believe is important and what you stand for. Make the product *communicate* . . . without compromise. The Sierra concept doesn't limit you to a single interpretation.

Symbolism is very important because we try to identify the potential clientele, a segment of the market, and the statement we made with the Sierra was a risky one. I like to get people interested in those cars so that they think of them as more than basic transport. Potentially this opens a new door for designers. Unfortunately, I think that for a fair number in that band of the market the amount of 'adjustment' we expected them to make was a bit more than they could initially digest. It was a concept statement, it was a more ambitious package of technology. Put that together and maybe people were not so much actively against, as a little bit afraid. The sales volume in Britain might have been disappointing, but with anything less we would not have been able to achieve our medium or long-term goals of re-establishing ourselves in the market-place.

Ex-Ford of Europe Chairman Bob Lutz admitted that with the Sierra the company was in a sense too ambitious:

We wanted to make the step from the adequate, cheap and cheerful and unadventurous cars to something which was making some demands on the customer.

92

It took nearly four years of customer acclimatization and a lot of me-too imitators before Sierra styling ceased to be a problem in Britain. In a different market sector, Audi had no such problem. It had a different one.

The Audi was promoted with a sophisticated press and television campaign using the Nazi tag, 'Vorsprung durch Technik' (Progress through Technology) . . . emblazoned like proud heraldry above their Ingolstadt factory gates. The Audi engineers are not self-indulgent men. One visitor to the factory says they are:

functional, but creative . . . their work environment is fascinating. It's pretty stripped down, but each of them has his trademark, a little luxury. A special telephone, for instance. They express their personality in a very restrained way. I suppose their cars are the same.

Audi used to retain Euro Advertising as its agency and, during the period when customers were perceived as sensitive about fuel economy at the expense of every other consideration, it had come up with the 'Drives like a six, drinks like a four' campaign to justify Audi's quirky choice of a five-cylinder engine for its flagship. The copywriter for this campaign had been Robin Wight, but when he left Euro Advertising to form his own agency (and, incidentally, to start writing copy for BMW ads), Audi-Volkswagen started looking around for another agency. Audi-Volkswagen's marketing man in the United Kingdom is a soft-spoken, charming, but intense and insistent Hungarian called John Meszadros. He had seen and admired John Hegarty's nostalgic Hovis ads on television and wanted something equally evocative for Audi. What Hegarty had done for Hovis, using picturesque streetscapes, sentimental music and a north-country voice-over, was to create an overwhelming impression of British 'goodness'. Now what they wanted was an overwhelming impression of German *Vorsprung*.

So Meszadros asked Bartle Bogle Hegarty to supply it.

Audi had become rich through its patents on the old NSU-Wankel rotary engine design. Although manufactured only by the Japanese Mazda company, every major car company felt it was going to need a rotary engine one day, so rights had been bought for all territories, netting Audi an estimated £50m a year. At the same time, the arrival of Ferry Porsche's son-in-law, Ferdinand Piech, in Ingolstadt from Stuttgart gave further encouragement to the development of a technically advanced new car.

As with Ford, Audi's research was beginning to show that consumers were now willing to accept aerodynamics as something relevant to their own purchase and not a technical nicety. The strategy for the advertising was to balance the rational choice of aerodynamics as a factor in car purchase, with other, more emotional factors. Britain is a unique market for selling cars, not only because of its unique media distribution, with the most sophisticated television advertising in the world, but also because of the curious national mood. In a culture which generally disdains technology as a worthwhile activity for its own citizens, British consumers clamour to buy foreign products which demonstrate a commitment to the stuff! Advertisers and marketing men know there is value in having something better, or in appearing to.

These national considerations meant that Audi marketing could ignore the European pilot advertising, agreed at the twice-yearly marketing meetings, and create a strategy for Britain alone. In Germany, Audis used to be bought by middle-ranking salesmen and small-town bank managers. The honest, white mac people you would ask for a favour, but never invite to dinner. Relocation . . .

For the consumer, technology is shorthand for 'my car is better than yours'. Audi underlined this emotional statement with the hardware to back it up: today the Audi

94

100 is the only car, except the Porsche 911 to which it is, in any case, culturally related, which has a galvanized body. Galvanizing, along with aerodynamics, full-time four wheel drive and turbocharging, was one of the annual 'technical events' which Piech planned when he joined Audi after the Porsche family bust-up. Originally planned at twelve-month intervals, Audi's appetite for innovation began to exhaust the available possibilities and now the events are occurring every eighteen months . . .

The philosophy, however, was there from the beginning. With its ancestry from Auto-Union, Horch and DKW, Audi is a cocktail of all the elements in the German automobile tradition and it is not too far-fetched to trace the history of the current cars back to the Auto-Unions which Hitler had Porsche design to demonstrate national technological supremacy. The company has always attracted some of the best engineers, and the cars have always attracted *rational* customers. First owners drive their Audis twice as far as BMWs. Consumer tests done in 1980 got the response 'Volkswagen, Mercedes, BMW' from people asked to name a German car. Audi 'had a miserable greyness which had to be polished'. Bartle Bogle Hegarty said it was 'entirely neutral, worthy'. The agency's research showed that some customers found Audi so faceless that they even thought they were made in Belgium! In June 1982 the median age of Audi drivers was 52.

According to Jeremy Judge, account director handling the Audi campaign, 'We didn't really exist as an advertising agency before we got Audi.' The fact that Robin Wight had left Euro Advertising and the Audi account and switched to BMW affected the British importers of Audi: 'They felt that this bloke's gone and done a good job on BMW. Perhaps we can take a risk on this bunch of people who have just started as well.' BBH was determined to sell the idea that people buy cars with their hearts as much as with their heads. Audi simply didn't have enough heart values going on . . . In Germany they were still being bought by customers who favoured the 'Jodelstil' of interior decoration with a *Schrankwand*, Bavarian scenes, overheating, overeating and shag pile.

Audi-Volkswagen wanted to use 'Vorsprung durch Technik' as a device to exploit the Audi inheritance, which was not well known in Britain. It was felt that the Latin imperative, Audi, (derived from the German imperative, *Horch*, the name of the founder) sounded too European and not German enough. In their part of the market it was good to be German and it was up to Hegarty to find a part of the 'pinhead to dance on': Porsche represented evolutionary engineering, Mercedes was quality engineering, BMW was driving engineering. BBH told Audi that they had to be about innovative engineering. Happily, this *aperçu* coincided with Audi's formidable range of new products. With their ads BBH located Audi as the *modern German car*.

BBH got moving in a hurry. Given the launch campaign for the new Audi 100 in autumn 1982, they got an idea about parachutes trailing behind the car as air brakes and, released one by one, rather like an aerodynamic version of Haydn's 'Farewell' Symphony, the slippery Audi would hustle on. Unfortunately, the Independent Television Contractors' Association insisted that they keep two parachutes on the car in order to demonstrate that Audis did in fact have *some* resistance to the air. The Association won and the ad was only a modest success. But then they got on with what they really wanted to do: add heart values to Audi.

BBH re-oriented Audi's advertising budget to television and away from the Press. This was on the face of it a curious decision, as only a very small percentage of the British market buys Audis: they only have to sell 23,000

At 70mph, the Audi 100 hardly moves.

The aerodynamics of the Audi 100 are as impressive from the side as they are from the front, so it's less susceptible to cross wind buffeting than virtually any other car. A comforting thought when you're about to pass a juggernaut on a wet motorway. Vorsprung durch Technik.

BEWARE CROSS WINDS

There have been three classic car advertising campaigns. In the fifties David Ogilvy wrote the copyline for Rolls-Royce which said at 60mph the loudest thing you can hear is the ticking of the clock; in the sixties Doyle Dane Bernbach's Volkswagen ads were masterpieces of accurately positioned understatement. The energy-conscious seventies saw no great campaigns, but in the mid-eighties London agency Bartle Bogle Hegarty created the successful and sophisticated 'Vorsprung durch Technik' television and press ads for Audi. The tag, curiously reminiscent of a Nazi slogan, brought the hitherto anonymous manufacturer to the attention of aspirational consumers with a taste for technology.

cars a year. An important part of the advertising campaign was to stimulate higher retained values and a key way of achieving this was, like Volvo, *to advertise to people who had already bought the cars.*

In a business environment with over-capacity and rapacious price-cutting, it was important for Audis to be heavily in demand and in short supply. BBH wanted to have the heart values so increased that demand kept the prices hard. The aim was to make people feel 'I want an Audi because it epitomizes the way I see myself', according to Jeremy Judge, Audi account director at the agency. He says:

You really want people to want the cars who aren't in the market this week, next year, or even the year after that: you're building an invisible attractiveness around Audi which is a reflection of social values. That's why we take care that the people in the ads are rather nice-looking and rather well-dressed and interesting. One hopes.

The problem here was: you can take the boy out of Germany, but you can't take Germany out of the boy. The creative problem was how to make the Audi appear more German, without making it seem humourless. The first television ads, 'Villas' and 'Gliders', achieve a mood of grave frivolity while dramatizing the German-ness, the style and the aspirational values of the new Audi:

Imagine a Spanish scene, a charming hill town. Voice-over:

Every year, the Schmidts, Müllers and the Reinhardts drive to their holiday villas

Cut to beautiful, turquoise swimming pool. Voice-over:

The Schmidts' car is rather slow and noisy, so when they arrive they'll need another holiday to get over this one

Cut to Spanish peasant woman locking gates, a classic exclusion motif. Cut to plodding donkey. Voice-over:

The Müllers drive a big, thirsty car, which is probably at a petrol station between Munich and Marbella

Cut to frog frisking in pool. Cut to Audi 100 parked in front of villa. Voice-over:

The Reinhardts drive an Audi 100, a car so aerodynamic it's capable of one hundred and twenty five miles per hour, yet at a steady fifty-six it will travel for seven hundred and fifty miles on one tank of petrol

Cut to impossibly leggy girl by pool. Voice-over:

And the moral of the story is, if you want to get to the beach before the Germans . . .

Cut to pair of Audis in a balletic intercourse.

You'd better buy an Audi 100. 'Vorsprung durch Technik' *as they say in Germany*

'Villas' became a cult, the sort of advertisement people discuss at dinner parties the way some people discuss feature films. Then Bartle Bogle Hegarty did an awful lot of research. They really knew the campaign was working because sales were climbing and soon after the campaign broke, younger people started buying Audis. But not everything was right, and they decided to sharpen the new image still further by excluding families from the Audi ads and focusing instead on the footloose singles who were their primary target. The succeeding ad, 'Gliders,' had a glamorous woman at the wheel of an Audi Quattro chasing her gliding man up a mountain to tell him that there was a call from his mother on his car phone. Art imitating life.

At the same time, Audi was winning rallies and BMW was busy diluting its own carefully wrought image by flooding the market with low-cost models now being driven by some very unlikely-looking people. On account of this, a managing director was fired. I imagine Audi's must have been promoted.

John Hegarty says:

Funnily enough, when you're doing advertising you always end up thinking that it will end sooner than it actually does because what happens is that as you live with it you learn that what you've got to do is take the Mick out of it much, much more. We've reached the point now where we've established it, we say 'Vorsprung durch Technik . . . *as they say in Germany*'. Now we've got to chuckle at that even more. We've got so say 'Come on, you know what we're trying to say. Let's not take this overly seriously.' By laughing we might even give it that something extra.

'Vorsprung durch Technik', Meszadros says, will last, if not for a thousand years, at least for another ten . . . At least, after Bartle Bogle Hegarty's efforts, the median age of Audi drivers has fallen to about 38. Which, in car marketing terms, is *exactly where you want to be*. With a mixture of technical events and extremely clever advertising, Audi cars were completely relocated in the marketplace. Technology combined with imagery to create not transport for salesmen, but intensely desirable costumes to be bought by the eager, young rich.

8 THE FUTURE
Zero Defects

A new industrial revolution will entail another revolution in aesthetics and design. The means of production inevitably dictate the character of the merchandise. With the new generation of intelligent machine tools, old assumptions about mass-production are blown apart. Instead of toiling to produce long runs of identical products, the factory of the future will be able to customize in units of one.

The car of the past is a complex product with many different meanings. If owning one is a 'parody of the act of love', then looking at one is a prologue to desire. Decade by decade, cars have reflected, then captured and then enhanced, the consumer's aspirations and tastes: from plutocratic to sexual display, through environmental concern to latter-day technophilia. More than any other manufactured product, the car enshrines and projects the values of the culture which created it: Ferraris *must* be red, a Mercedes-Benz *has* to be the colour of hard metal, not of crushed soft fruit.

But what of the car of the future? In a world where the economic and industrial assumptions which made Henry Ford's first mass-produced car possible, a new industrial revolution, with its origins in the orient, is changing our patterns of work and patterns of consumption.

The first structural shift in industrial production which allowed design changes to be made was Ford's combination of assembly-line construction with Frederick Taylor's man-management science. Adapted for a bigger stage by Alfred Sloan's General Motors, mass-production introduced the world to uniform products. The second shift occurred in Europe after the Second World War with a flurry of developments (including light structures, disc brakes, front wheel drive) which brought about the technically advanced small car. The third shift has happened recently in Japan, where after years of aping European and American design while getting their factories sorted, process efficiency is at such a level that 'zero defects' is not a distant goal, but an everyday reality.

The Japanese first improvised little cars out of
motor-bike components, then spent a lot of time
aping Western norms while they sorted out the
process efficiency of their factories. By the
mid-eighties they were near to achieving 'zero
defects' in production, while the perfection of their
manufacturing system allowed them to innovate
freely and frequently. The Nissan Cue-X, shown
at the 1985 Tokyo Motor Show, is still in touch
with Western norms, but it is inevitable that in the
future the Japanese will develop a symbolic
language that is entirely novel.

There is a dynamic which is built into the production process in Japan. When the Japanese decided to take on the West's automobile industry, they started in all humility, at least in design terms. They bought licences to produce the British Austin 7 and the French Renault. They hired designers from California, so their sports cars would look right. They shamelessly imitated momentary fashions in Euro-American styling and concentrated instead in getting the metal out of the factory. With a characteristically oriental taste for reduction, they dramatically cut stock levels in their factories and created their *kan-ban* (just-in-time) system of production. With no glut of expensive stocks, production became cheaper in unit terms, but more important, taking the gluts out of the system allowed them to isolate bottlenecks which, one by one, they extirpated. This process created the most ergonomically and economically functional factories on earth. The Japanese can conceive, design, tool for and manufacture an entire new engine in about the time it takes a comparable European or American company to think about having lunch. The fourth shift is happening today, as the Japanese look for something else to achieve, now that they have mastered industrial production.

The process of making (and later, of selling) cars is changing rapidly, but the taste for symbolism, as ineradicable in human beings as the parallel appetites for love and sustenance, is going to stick around. The big question is: now that the Japanese are poised to dominate the world markets, how will they design cars for the emotional needs of alien cultures and how will the remaining, embattled and embittered, European and American manufacturers respond?

An international body of academics has been studying the car of the future. I asked Dan Jones, one of its leaders, how the study came about:

The International Automobile Programme came about because people were concerned about urban congestion and transportation problems and, according to the wisdom of the seventies, the car was doomed in cities. The members of the programme realized that if they were going to study the automobile, they were going to have to study the automobile industry as well. As we got into the project it became very clear that the major issue actually wasn't congestion because a lot of things had happened to make that more manageable. The real issue was an emerging trade conflict between a super-competitive Japanese industry and the rest of the world which was reeling from this new competitive shock which it didn't really understand.

The original thesis of the IAP investigation was made invalid: by technical developments arising out of the oil shocks—weight-loss, aerodynamics, more efficient engines—and by the inventiveness of the Japanese. The direct outcome of these accumulated benefits was that, by 1982, cars like the Audi 100 and Ford Sierra stood on their heads most of the old assumptions about mass-market cars. In marketing terms, people began to advertise technology and the Japanese, in a pattern seen with their motor-bikes, cameras, hi-fis, videos and now with their cars, were determined to sell more and more technology. This competitiveness has had a profound effect on the style, character and design of cars because people realized that 'there's a lot of stretch left in conventional cars'. It's that stretch that's being exploited now.

With their completely different technique of managing industrial activity the Japanese have dominated production of cheap, low-margin cars. The only way for the Europeans and Americans to compete is to specialize: in the United States Chrysler is planning 'niche production' aiming to produce each of its models in runs of no more than 100–150,000 and recently even considered buying

BMW, that most 'specialist' of manufacturers; it already co-produces cars with Italy's Maserati.

This means the end of the temporarily fashionable 'globalization' concept, touted by Harvard Business School's well-publicized pundit, Theodore Levitt. Although in his book *The Marketing Imagination* (1983) Levitt claims to detect 'a general drift towards world homogenization', more recently observers with a keener eye for product see quite the opposite thing happening. In an article in *Marxism Today*, published at the beginning of 1986, Dan Jones said:

With little sign of demand patterns converging within or between countries the era of the large volume 'world car', if it ever existed, may now be over.

The Japanese wiped out the viability of the Euro-American world car by their awesome efficiency. It is exactly this form of industrial efficiency which puts them into a position to exploit the fragmentation of world markets. In global terms, market segmentation is increasing. It's all getting more complex and, according to Phil Gardiner of The Science Policy Research Unit, Sussex University's think tank, 'It's scaring the shit out of manufacturers'.

Ford's 'AJ' programme was a response to this, but a visit to the latest Tokyo Motor Show demonstrates that, no matter how brave in its time, the Ford Sierra was a naive response to what is for Western civilization a very big problem. The order-of-magnitude changes that are going on are signalling something very significant: the Japanese are researching the 'whole portfolio of available technology'. Patenting activity is a clear indication of the volume of research and development taking place and, recently, Germany and Japan have pushed the United States into third place in the global patenting league.

Significantly, the number of Japanese patents lodged abroad has grown rapidly and continues to increase.

Dan Jones says 'We've just seen the *beginning* of the Japanese' . . . because as Western manufacturers learn from the just-in-time systems of inventory control and learn to get the product quality control right, the Japanese are preparing the next phase of their attack on Western industry: dramatically increasing the technological content and the consumer options and the design in their cars. No European or American manufacturer who couldn't get *kan-ban* and quality right is even going to have a *chance* of competing as the next wave of oriental innovation comes in. Once it was said that America led the world in marketing, Europe in technology and the Japanese in process efficiency. Not since the pioneering years of Henry Ford has anybody led the world in all three areas . . . until now and the leader is Japan.

The problem is how to cope with complexity on a mass-production basis. The current range of Honda Civics shows the way: four different cars on one platform. You can only see the depth of Honda's influence in the United States because European quotas distort the picture of the real penetration of Japanese cars into Western markets. The Japanese have learnt how to use design. At first they copied Europe, but their culture's traditional reverence for flat, graphic forms made their cars awkward when seen as three-dimensional objects: early Toyotas and Datsuns were unhappy reminders that the Japanese have no tradition of monumental sculpture (even if some of the gloriously baroque mouldings on cars of the sixties recalled the grotesque distortions of that other traditional art form, *kabuki*). Later Japanese manufacturers used American exiles to design their sports cars and hired the Italian *carroziere* – including Michelotti and ItalDesign – to do their more mundane cars. By the eighties they had learnt all the tricks themselves and their sophistication in CAD-CAM techniques gave them astonishing flexibility and speed in innovation.

Now that the envelope and the inner environment of every Japanese car is styled up to the nine-pins, they are seeking more ways to exploit the consumer's appetite for design. Already, in an amusing extension of the idea of 'conspicuous' consumption, they are styling those areas of cars – suspension towers and engine bays, for instance – which had hitherto been *invisible*. As they continue to push on with their domination of world markets, it is conceivable that one day soon every component of a Datsun or a Toyota will be as highly styled as dashboards, hub caps and rear light clusters used to be.

The Europeans can't even guess what's going to come next, according to Andy Graves of The Science Policy Research Unit, because in Japan it comes out of the manufacturing process itself, out of the factory. The designs are often tidied up at the product stage because the technology they use to manufacture is forcing them to do that. They don't try to second guess: they keep on and on trying . . . it comes out of the floorboards. They don't lick problems at the end of the line, they just don't have problems. The Western tradition of competitive individualism cannot cope with the Japanese threat.

How will these Japanese cars affect the manners and habits of libidinous Western youth and would-be libidinous Western middle-class consumers? When the Japanese have run out of Western ideas to parody and exploit, what ideas will they then put into new cars? What will be the source of the new symbols?

Perhaps cars will become less like capital equipment and more like consumer durables. Already, there is very little difference between a Suzuki Alto and a kitchen appliance like a micro-wave oven. Similarly, as a stockbroker's report has recently suggested, perhaps cars will be sold in supermarkets. Segmentation of the market will be expressed in cars with modular interiors: you will be able to buy a 'shell' and then select mission-adaptable modules, from a wide range of options which might, just conceivably, be branded with non-automotive names: Benetton, Next, Levis, Coca-Cola. These modules might include not only the necessary instrumentation and control systems for the vehicle's operation, but also increasingly sophisticated audio and video devices, together with personal care accessories. This promised flexibility of the new car interior will mean that after-market specialists will become fully integrated into the new car purchasing cycle: the fifth shift in automotive technology will be the reconciliation of hitherto distinct 'disciplines' of information science, ergonomics and textiles into automobile design.

Uwe Bahnsen, head of Ford of Europe's design department, explains some of his thinking:

Today's consumer is more interested in overall product integrity rather than just the cheapest buy on the High Street. I can't imagine somebody being interested in a modern hi-fi set going out and buying a Cortina. They just don't go together. People are becoming more discerning.

Uwe Bahnsen has this idea of reversing some of the assumptions about construction, using a plastic frame with steel panels bonded to the plastic.

It offers fascinating perspectives for integrating structure and function within one component. All the elements of structure can be formulated to the nth degree. You can forget about plastic's susceptibility to chemicals, but you can integrate into the plastic frame all the ducting and can provide dedicated channels for all the electrical equipment . . . so that there are fantastic opportunities to have the frame perform the functions which are presently installed only *after* major assembly has been completed.

The foregoing nice discussions of style may well be upstaged by technical developments coming from aerospace. Already the European A320 Airbus has controls which dispense with the mechanical-hydraulic linkages which connect the pilot's hand to the flying surfaces. More radical still, McDonnell-Douglas in the United States are developing bio-cybernetic systems which will one day allow the aeroplane to translate the pilot's *thoughts* into actions performed by the plane. Innovations in aerospace have traditionally found their way into car design and, already, the Japanese have wall-to-wall electronics, distance sensors and are discussing satellite navigation systems as a building-block for the driverless car they are so anxious to achieve.

But how far can you go on *selling* technology? The horse-power race ran out of steam, people got bored with experimental safety vehicles; even Audi had to postpone its technical events to once every eighteen months. Perhaps the next breakthrough will be the genuinely innovative *simple car*. The simple car will come about from designing from the inside out: not adding electronics to existing systems, but designing something completely new. These changes would create a threshold. The end of incremental changes and a new set of bases for the car of the future.

The zero-defect, driverless car idea might appeal to the oriental taste for perfection and order, but history and experience suggest that, like people, cars have to be flawed to be interesting. No matter what technology is available, unless a car is carrying a load of effective imagery it is unlikely to enjoy genuine popular success. In the past, that imagery has come in morphology derived either from aircraft, or busts, bottoms and the other pleats, tucks, depressions and protuberances of the body.

The driverless car might appeal to an industrial system,

like Japan's, which requires regular incremental applications of technology, but it has less appeal in Western cultures where a persistent element in erotic fantasy is making love with a stranger. Driving is something akin. The German architect, Peter Behrens, thought that 'a motor should be like a birthday present'. Harley Earl designed his cars so that every time you got in one it was like having 'a little vacation'. The release into a fantasy world promised by a fast car is like the promised release integral with active sex. Perhaps most important, the freedom and dynamism of the car, to say nothing of its external beauty and the quality of its interior, is a vindication of the dreams of the Futurists and the rhapsodic vapourings of the founders of the Modern Movement in architecture and design.

The funny thing is, if you choose, you can enjoy it now . . . while it's still got the defects!

For permission to use quotations and extracts, the publishers gratefully acknowledge the following:

A noted authority on graphic arts, Stephen Bayley is director of the design wing of the Victoria and Albert Museum in London. He is also the author of several books, including *Harley Earl and the Dream Machine*, and has contributed articles to a wide variety of British publications.